I0015573

Learning Splunk Web Framework

Take your analytics online with the ease and power of the Splunk Web Framework

Vincent Sesto

BIRMINGHAM - MUMBAI

Learning Splunk Web Framework

Copyright © 2016 Packt Publishing

All rights reserved. No part of this book may be reproduced, stored in a retrieval system, or transmitted in any form or by any means, without the prior written permission of the publisher, except in the case of brief quotations embedded in critical articles or reviews.

Every effort has been made in the preparation of this book to ensure the accuracy of the information presented. However, the information contained in this book is sold without warranty, either express or implied. Neither the author, nor Packt Publishing, and its dealers and distributors will be held liable for any damages caused or alleged to be caused directly or indirectly by this book.

Packt Publishing has endeavored to provide trademark information about all of the companies and products mentioned in this book by the appropriate use of capitals. However, Packt Publishing cannot guarantee the accuracy of this information.

First published: August 2016

Production reference: 1260816

Published by Packt Publishing Ltd.
Livery Place
35 Livery Street
Birmingham
B3 2PB, UK.
ISBN 978-1-78646-294-7

www.packtpub.com

Credits

Author

Vincent Sesto

Copy Editor

Vikrant Phadke

Reviewer

Robert King

Project Coordinator

Nidhi Joshi

Commissioning Editor

Julian Ursell

Proofreader

Safis Editing

Acquisition Editor

Manish Nainani

Indexer

Mariammal Chettiyar

Content Development Editor

Mayur Pawanikar

Graphics

Disha Haria

Technical Editor

Mohita Vyas

Production Coordinator

Arvindkumar Gupta

About the Author

Vincent Sesto, when changing skill sets and moving from business into the information technology field 10 years ago, saw the potential of doing things via technology and has continued to follow his passion to find better ways of doing so. Vince has worked with Splunk for the past 4 years, developing apps and reporting applications around Splunk, and now works hard to advocate its success. He has worked as a system engineer in big data companies and development departments, where he has regularly supported, built, and developed with Splunk. His LinkedIn profile is at `https://au.linkedin.com/in/vincesesto`.

About the Reviewer

Robert King has primarily served as an engineer, writing desktop, client-server, and web software in more languages than he can remember, and has been building human-computer interfaces for longer than he cares to admit. Although he has also served as sysadmin and DBA, for the last decade he has focused primarily on web-based frontend development, having built experiences used by millions of customers everyday.

www.PacktPub.com

For support files and downloads related to your book, please visit www.PacktPub.com.

eBooks, discount offers, and more

Did you know that Packt offers eBook versions of every book published, with PDF and ePub files available? You can upgrade to the eBook version at www.PacktPub.com and as a print book customer, you are entitled to a discount on the eBook copy. Get in touch with us at customercare@packtpub.com for more details.

At www.PacktPub.com, you can also read a collection of free technical articles, sign up for a range of free newsletters and receive exclusive discounts and offers on Packt books and eBooks.

https://www2.packtpub.com/books/subscription/packtlib

Do you need instant solutions to your IT questions? PacktLib is Packt's online digital book library. Here, you can search, access, and read Packt's entire library of books.

Why subscribe?

- Fully searchable across every book published by Packt
- Copy and paste, print, and bookmark content
- On demand and accessible via a web browser

Free access for Packt account holders

Get notified! Find out when new books are published by following @PacktEnterprise on Twitter or the Packt Enterprise Facebook page.

Table of Contents

Preface

For some time now, Splunk has been a leading light in providing software that allows its users to search, monitor, and visualize data. The massive expansion in machine data seems endless but we are fortunate to have the tools to deliver and analyze this data and allow us to strip out the irrelevant information, presenting to our user base the important data that will help guide business and technology decisions. Two major strengths that Splunk provides are the ability to quickly analyze your data as well as the ability to present this information to your user in an attractive and customizable way. This presentation layer sitting within Splunk as part of the Splunk Web Framework is a powerful development platform from which we can almost endlessly customize the data we are providing. This book focuses directly on the Splunk Web Framework. It is designed to provide hands-on and interesting examples with step-by-step instructions, to help developers think of Splunk as a complete platform instead of software for searching, monitoring, and analyzing machine-generated data. This book provides different and interesting examples instead of the usual "Log, Index, Search, and Graph" and has the reader thinking in terms of Splunk being the first tool they think of when needing to resolve any problem.

What this book covers

Chapter 1, *Splunk Web Framework Fundamentals*, provides a high-level overview of the framework as well as discussing development environments and collaborating with development teams.

Chapter 2, *Presenting Data to Users as a Splunk App*, will introduce Splunk Apps and get you to use the Web Interface to create basic dashboards to present their data.

Chapter 3, *Expand Your Apps Using Simple XML*, expands you knowledge of Splunk App development by introducing Simple XML to manipulate the underlying dashboard code.

Chapter 4, *Layouts, Navigation, and Menus*, provides you with an overview of how to use Simple XML to control the layout of you dashboards as well as setting up a menu system for you Splunk App.

Chapter 5, *Interacting with Your User While Speeding Up App Searches*, discusses how to add features to your Simple XML code to allow your user to interact directly with their Splunk data.

Chapter 6, *Moving from Simple XML to HTML*, introduces HTML dashboards and provides an explanation of the HTML code that is generated as part of the Splunk dashboard.

Chapter 7, *JavaScript Modules in Your HTML App*, provides a discussion on how to work directly with JavaScript modules in your Splunk App to further enhance functionality.

Chapter 8, *Utilizing CSS to Spice Up Visual Appeal*, discusses working directly with CSS files to manipulate the look and feel of a dashboard and move away from the standard Splunk color scheme.

Chapter 9, *Moving Your App off Splunk with SplunkJS*, provides an in-depth introduction to using SplunkJS to create standalone web applications with the use of Splunk data.

What you need for this book

To be able to work along with the example applications created in this book, you will need to have the following items available:

- A running version of Splunk Enterprise, preferably on Linux or Mac
- Basic knowledge of Splunk and how it works, including creating searches and reports, indexing data, and knowledge of Web interface
- A modern and stable web browser, such as Chrome or Firefox
- A basic understanding of web technologies such as HTML, CSS, and JavaScript
- Some basic knowledge of Python
- An Internet connection

Who this book is for

This book is designed to start from an overview of the Splunk Web framework and get an inexperienced Splunk user to work fast with hands-on examples. The examples build on top of each other to cover more advanced topics, so it is hoped that even an experienced Splunk developer will be able to get something out of this book as the chapters progress.

Conventions

In this book, you will find a number of text styles that distinguish between different kinds of information. Here are some examples of these styles and an explanation of their meaning.

Code words in text, database table names, folder names, filenames, file extensions, pathnames, dummy URLs, user input, and Twitter handles are shown as follows: "By clicking on the Splunk logo at the top left of the screen, we are brought to the home page, `http://localhost:8000/en-GB/app/launcher/home`."

A block of code is set as follows:

```
1 <dashboard>
2   <label>SimpleXMLDashboard</label>
```

Any command-line input or output is written as follows:

```
echo "# SplunkAppDev" >> README.md
```

New terms and **important words** are shown in bold.

Warnings or important notes appear in a box like this.

Tips and tricks appear like this.

For this book we have outlined the shortcuts for the Mac OX platform if you are using the Windows version you can find the relevant shortcuts on the WebStorm help page `https://www.jetbrains.com/webstorm/help/keyboard-shortcuts-by-category.html`.

Reader feedback

Feedback from our readers is always welcome. Let us know what you think about this book—what you liked or disliked. Reader feedback is important for us as it helps us develop titles that you will really get the most out of.

To send us general feedback, simply e-mail `feedback@packtpub.com`, and mention the book's title in the subject of your message.

If there is a topic that you have expertise in and you are interested in either writing or contributing to a book, see our author guide at `www.packtpub.com/authors`.

Customer support

Now that you are the proud owner of a Packt book, we have a number of things to help you to get the most from your purchase.

Downloading the example code

You can download the example code files for this book from your account at `http://www.p acktpub.com`. If you purchased this book elsewhere, you can visit `http://www.packtpub.c om/support` and register to have the files e-mailed directly to you.

You can download the code files by following these steps:

1. Log in or register to our website using your e-mail address and password.
2. Hover the mouse pointer on the **SUPPORT** tab at the top.
3. Click on **Code Downloads & Errata**.
4. Enter the name of the book in the **Search** box.
5. Select the book for which you're looking to download the code files.
6. Choose from the drop-down menu where you purchased this book from.
7. Click on **Code Download**.

You can also download the code files by clicking on the **Code Files** button on the book's webpage at the Packt Publishing website. This page can be accessed by entering the book's name in the Search box. Please note that you need to be logged in to your Packt account.

Once the file is downloaded, please make sure that you unzip or extract the folder using the latest version of:

- WinRAR / 7-Zip for Windows
- Zipeg / iZip / UnRarX for Mac
- 7-Zip / PeaZip for Linux

Downloading the color images of this book

We also provide you with a PDF file that has color images of the screenshots/diagrams used in this book. The color images will help you better understand the changes in the output. You can download this file from `https://www.packtpub.com/sites/default/files/down loads/ApexDesignPatterns_ColorImages.pdf`.

Errata

Although we have taken every care to ensure the accuracy of our content, mistakes do happen. If you find a mistake in one of our books—maybe a mistake in the text or the code—we would be grateful if you could report this to us. By doing so, you can save other readers from frustration and help us improve subsequent versions of this book. If you find any errata, please report them by visiting http://www.packtpub.com/submit-errata, selecting your book, clicking on the **Errata Submission Form** link, and entering the details of your errata. Once your errata are verified, your submission will be accepted and the errata will be uploaded to our website or added to any list of existing errata under the Errata section of that title.

To view the previously submitted errata, go to https://www.packtpub.com/books/content/support and enter the name of the book in the search field. The required information will appear under the **Errata** section.

Piracy

Piracy of copyrighted material on the Internet is an ongoing problem across all media. At Packt, we take the protection of our copyright and licenses very seriously. If you come across any illegal copies of our works in any form on the Internet, please provide us with the location address or website name immediately so that we can pursue a remedy.

Please contact us at copyright@packtpub.com with a link to the suspected pirated material.

We appreciate your help in protecting our authors and our ability to bring you valuable content.

Questions

If you have a problem with any aspect of this book, you can contact us at questions@packtpub.com, and we will do our best to address the problem.

1
Splunk Web Framework Fundamentals

My history with Splunk goes back about 4 years to when I was working for a company that was building a browser plugin. All of the logging for all the users was going to be built around Splunk. I am not sure whether they knew the implications, but it was not until some 2 years later that I saw the full benefit of making this decision. I had been convinced of the power of Splunk. I saw it as a great platform to build and develop applications and reports with ease, and it should be looked at in exactly the same way as LAMP or other development stacks. I also saw the opportunity to write a book about the Splunk Web Framework as a great way to show other people what I have learned without them having to waste the time of trial and error that I had to.

If you have not yet installed Splunk on a virtual machine, server, or your own PC or laptop, it is probably best to get this done now before moving further. Towards the end of this chapter, we will introduce the data and example projects that we will be working on throughout this book. The example work that we will be performing throughout this book will be on a Linux or Mac platform. You should be able to follow along if you are using a different platform. If you have not installed Splunk before, you will be able to get all the details you need for your installation at the following link: `http://docs.splunk.com/Docu`
`mentation/Splunk/6.3.3/Installation/Chooseyourplatform`.

So you've installed Splunk, got things running, and now what? Hopefully, that is where this book will come in and help you get the ball rolling, making fresh, interactive, useful, and dynamic applications using the Splunk Web Framework. We are hoping that we can actually get you creating some interesting applications without the usual log, index, search, graph, and report documentation that seems to be out in abundance.

Introducing the Splunk Web Framework

Welcome to the Splunk Web Framework, which has been set up as an essential support structure for Splunkusers to build custom reports, dashboards, and apps on Splunk and with Splunk. This means that there is a supporting environment that can be used to develop end-to-end applications with no need to install anything other than Splunk. The Splunk Web Framework allows the user to start from the basics using a drag-and-drop interface, and makes them able to get underneath the hood and interact and customize the code directly. Further still, developers don't even need to develop with Splunk as their platform of choice to display their data. They are free to simply interface with Splunk API calls, search for data, and then display this returned data directly on their own websites and applications.

As of Splunk version 6, there was a major overhaul to the Splunk Web Framework. The framework is now integrated directly into Splunk Enterprise 6, so now you don't need to install anything else to start using the web framework. Previously, in Splunk 5, you needed to use a standalone version of the web framework. So unless you're using an old version of Splunk, you will be able to get going and working with the framework straight away. All your apps from previous versions of Splunk should work on Splunk 6, including apps created in Advanced XML, so it is well worth the upgrade to get an improved interface and functionality that it brings.

A quick note about advanced XML

Let's get this out of the way early. You may have heard about Advanced XML, or you may have even seen some dashboards or views created in your environment that have been set up using Advanced XML. As of Splunk Enterprise 6.3, the Advanced XML feature has been deprecated. Although apps and dashboards using Advanced XML will continue to work and Splunk will continue to support and fix bugs, there will no longer be any feature enhancements to the Advanced XML feature of the Splunk Web Framework.

A date has not yet been set for the removal of Advanced XML from Splunk Enterprise. All future development should be done using other features of the Splunk Web Framework, and all existing apps or dashboards that use Advanced XML should be migrated away from Advanced XML and onto one of the other options available in the Splunk Web Framework.

All the examples and work in this book will be using Splunk version 6.4, so we will not be performing any of the example exercises in Advanced XML. When we start to develop with Splunk's XML code, the only approach we will take towards Advanced XML will be to show you how to recognize applications made with Advanced XML.

Architecture of the Splunk Web Framework

The Splunk Web Framework is now built directly on the core Splunk daemon, splunkd. Originally, splunkd only handled indexing, searching, and forwarding, but as of version 6.2, it also operates the Splunk Web Interface. Making this change was practical because it gave the framework the tools you need to build web applications directly on Splunk, as well as use the data that Splunk provides to display on your own website.

Within the framework, you have an app that will include numerous dashboard elements within the app. Within the dashboards, you will then have numerous panel and visualization elements that will make up your dashboard:

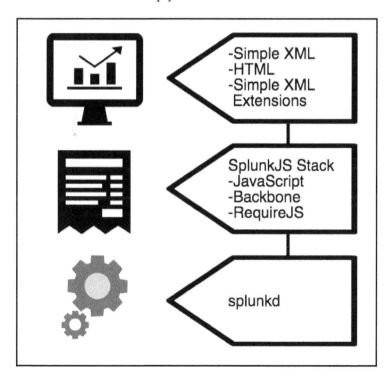

Description of the architecture

The preceding diagram provides a clear breakdown of the architecture, and its three distinct layers. It shows splunkd, which is built on C/C++ for speed and stability, as a server that provides the indexing and searching capabilities to the SplunkJS stack, which delivers the display and interface supporting the SimpleXML, HTML, and external web displays. Each layer builds on the others, providing further enhanced functionality.

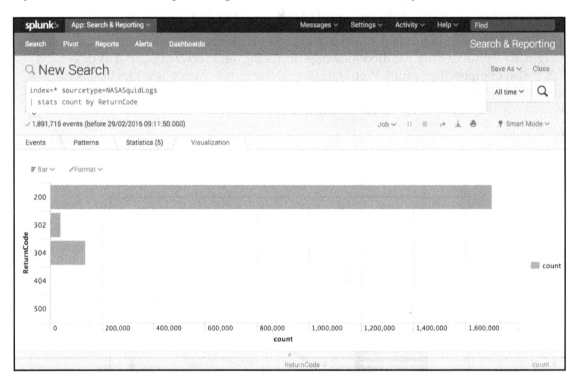

The Splunk web interface

By now, I am sure you at least know that Splunk has a web interface. If you are competent with using Splunk, you would already be familiar with using the web interface for searching, configuring, and administration of Splunk. As part of the Splunk Web Framework, the web interface also provides an easy-to-use graphical user interface, which allows you to drag and drop tools and functionality with no prior programming knowledge or experience. It provides rapid development on the framework and allows you to visualize dashboard panels with ease.

The dashboard editor is the main interface and is part of the SimpleXML layer of the Splunk Web Framework; it allows you to build dashboards within Splunk Web. Here you can visualize your events and statistical information as dashboard panels and views and provide charting functionality. It even allows you to start providing form-based controls and an interface with the user.

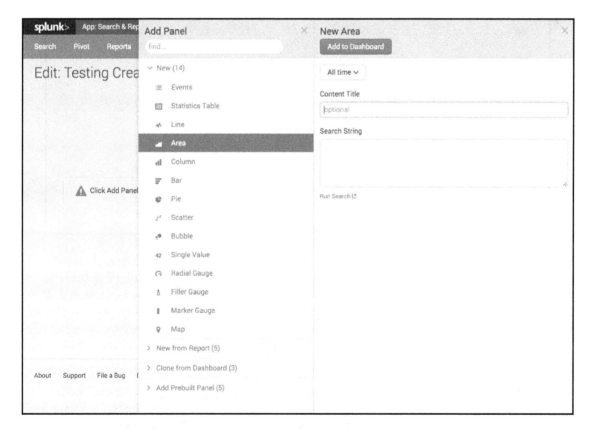

Simple XML

Simple XML expands the functionality of the framework further and allows the user to fine-tune the dashboard panels with more layout and display options. Splunk's **Extensible Markup Language** (**XML**) is the underlying code that is developed when using the web interface and dashboard editor. Simple XML code can be edited and manipulated directly from Splunk's built-in editor, or you can use your own code editor to configure the easy-to-learn syntax. The directory structure within Splunk is also straightforward and easy to learn, and it helps you manipulate the environment in ways that you can't actually do within the web interface.

From the preceding example, you can see that the syntax of the Simple XML code is straightforward and relatively easy to learn. The code provides a multitude of options to tweak and fine-tune all aspects of the display of the different types of panels provided. It is definitely worth learning to use this function of the Splunk Web Framework. Although the drag-and-drop interface allows you to develop rich and interesting dashboard panels, sooner or later you will start to want to configure the display in a way that you can only do in SimpleXML.

Each visualization type has a long list of properties that can be managed and changed through SimpleXML code. Although simple, you still need to adhere to the white space and open and close tags within the code. If not, you could end up with no display provided.

SimpleXML extensions

SimpleXML also allows you to create extensions to utilize CSS and JavaScript files so that you can further modify and enhance the behavior and appearance of a dashboard that was created through the code editor or web interface. You can modify the layouts further, add new visualizations, and customize the way that the end user interacts with the dashboards.

Working with SimpleXML extensions will get you working directly in the server directory structure of your Splunk deployment. Once you have added your CSS or JavaScript files to the server, it is simply a matter of editing your code to then use the files needed.

HTML

By now, you can see that each level of the framework expands functionality of the interface further, and utilizing HTML dashboards allows you to expand your functionality even further. Splunk comes with a converter that allows you to convert your Simple XML dashboards into HTML, and allows you to use the built-in code editor, edit, and configure the HTML dashboard further. As with Simple XML, you are also able to use your favorite code editor, allowing developers with knowledge of HTML, CSS, and JavaScript to transfer their knowledge and work directly in Splunk by using it as a platform to generate their HTML-based environment.

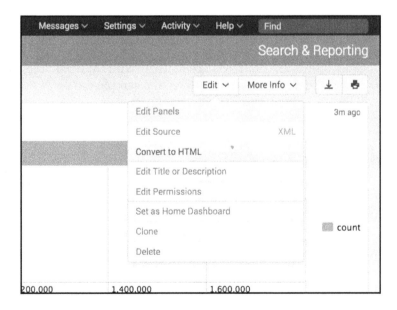

SplunkJS libraries

`SplunkJS` provides a framework of tools and libraries that allows developers to build and manage dashboards and organize dependencies, as well as integrate Splunk components into their own web applications. The libraries allow you to manage views and search managers to allow you to work with searches and interact with Splunk data. `SplunkJS` removes the developer from the Splunk Web Interface but gives the ability to both build Splunk Apps for Splunk and build web applications using Splunk data.

splunkd

This is the main system process that Splunk uses to handle all of the indexing, searching, forwarding, and web interface that you work with in Splunk Enterprise. Although we will need to restart Splunk and the splunkd process occasionally, this book will not be focusing on splunkd, as this would be more of a server administration focus.

The development process and development environment

For the next few pages, we are going to take a little break from Splunk and specifically look at the development process and using Git as part of this process. The topics covered are more suited to new developers or developers who are not familiar with working as part of a team or with applications such as Git. If you are familiar with these subjects, feel free to jump to the end of this chapter, where we introduce the sample data and example applications we will be working on through this book.

The development process

When you work in a team developing applications, there is most likely a process in place that you would need to follow to develop, deploy to the development environment, test, deploy to the test environment, test, and deploy to production. It sounds like a lot of work, but the last thing you want to be doing is deploy a new application into a production environment and realize that you have misspelled the company name, or worse still, you are getting the following dreaded *no show* screen from Splunk.

This book is not designed to educate you on the software development process, and there are many books, videos, and courses dedicated to the subject, but we will go through a brief run through of the types of things you should be thinking about and the types of good habits you should be getting into.

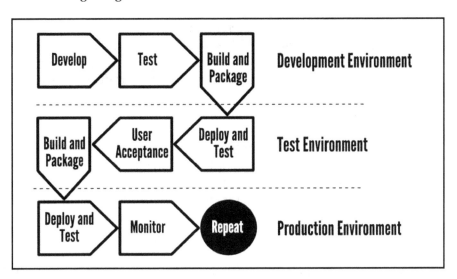

So, even if you are just developing at home on your own projects, it is good practice to get into the habit of setting up and following a development process, including using a specific development host that mirrors the setup of the production server and some form of version control software:

- Develop your application in your development environment. Even if your development environment is on your laptop or PC, you need to make sure that you are developing on an identical environment to what your application will be eventually deployed on. You won't be able to have everything 100%, but you need to make sure you are using the same language versions and libraries and on the same operating system.
- Test your application in your development environment. Within Agile development methodologies, we can perform test-driven development, where the writing of tests should be performed at the start of the development process. As each iteration of your application is completed, you then need to implement these tests to verify the operation of your application and lodge any bugs or defects that may be found after the development process.

- In the preceding diagram, we showed that we are packaging our application. For now, we will be using Git as part of our development process instead of packaging our application before release. In later chapters, we will also take a look at packaging our Splunk app to deploy and allow others to use our application.

- Deploy your application in a test environment. This is only after your application has successfully passed testing. This should be a standalone environment, isolated from development and once again set up to mimic your production setup. A test environment should go further than your development environment to mimic how the application will be run in production. It should even be on the same hardware as well as operating systems and have the same accompanying applications.

- Test your application in a test environment. Upon successful deployment in your test environment, you can test the application further. It is not a matter of simply performing the same tests that you did in development. This is your chance to perform security tests, make sure that the performance of the application and surrounding applications that are on the same environment is also fine, and simulate production loads to ensure that your application operates under heavy usage.

- User acceptance testing. If you are working for a specific client, you may be asking them to access the application deployed in the test environment and make sure that it operates to their agreed-upon standard. This may mean that the client has requested specific features be added and bugs be removed. If user acceptance testing is in place for your development process, this will usually be the final approval before it is deployed to production.

- Deploy to production. It's time to push the button and deploy your changes into production. If everything has worked as it should, you shouldn't have any surprises, but it is still important to test your application as you would to make sure that the functionality of your application still works the way it should.

- Monitor a new application in production. We're working with Splunk aren't we? Well, this is where we can set up monitoring for our application to make sure we are not seeing an increase in errors, a decline in usage, weird things happening with our hardware and unauthorized users accessing our application.

In the early stages of development of an application, the development process can be stripped down a little. Your production environment may be running on your laptop, but still keep the aforementioned processes in mind so that when you move on to developing within more complex environments and architectures, you will have the basics covered and extending them will not be too difficult.

Development environment

You should have a development environment set up as closely as possible to mirror what you are deploying in production. If you need to set up VirtualBox, VMware, or another virtualization environment, it is worth doing so to make sure you are setting up an operating system—the same as what you have in production. At the very least, your version of Splunk should be the exact same version as what you will be deploying in production.

Nowadays, with products such as Amazon Web Services, Google Cloud, and Softlayer from IBM, they offer us a much easier way to create development, test, and production environments that all mirror each other without the need to interact with hardware. Automation can also be put in place to create the environment, deploy code, and then test against that environment. Within later chapters of this book, we will touch on automated testing, packaging, and deployment of our code, but for now, we will use collaboration tools such as source code management software to allow us to deploy our code in development and in turn revert changes when needed.

Data to test with

It may not be possible to have the data indexed in exactly the same way as you would be able to in production, but ensure that you have a sample to demonstrate that visualizations and reports are operating correctly and will provide the insight that you need. Try to have as much data as you can, as with reporting tools such as Splunk, your development process may need to incorporate speeding up and optimization of your searches.

Using collaboration tools... enter Git

When discussing the development process, it's probably the best time to introduce collaboration tools such as Git to help you manage your code and track changes. Git is a free and open source tool that offers source code management and collaboration features that should hopefully improve the way we code and interact with our code. As a developer working on smaller projects and development environments, you may be tempted to simply make the changes locally and upload your work to a web server when you're done, but by using source code management software such as Git, you are able to do the following:

- Track and monitor changes to your code. Even if you are working alone on a project, Git will allow you keep a historical log of all the changes made to your code. You may find non-developers accessing code on production environments and making changes to code. Git allows you to verify that the code has not been altered from the original source code. Disk space is not over-utilized in the process as Git only keeps a copy of the changes made and not an entire copy of the software each time changes are made.

- Create specific versions of projects. This allows you to demonstrate changes over time to keep track of feature enhancements to your code and bug fixes, and allows you to easily establish when bugs may have entered your code.

- Revert to old versions of code. As you have been creating versions of your software and tracking your changes, it then becomes a lot easier to back out of changes or revert to old versions of code if something goes wrong. As long as your servers have Git installed and can access your repository, changes can be deployed or reverted with ease and pushed onto each of your development and production environments.

- It allows you to collaborate with other developers. Features and projects can be branched off, so development can be performed on the same code by numerous developers and then merged back once the development is complete. Git also allows these projects to be updated from the central code base on a periodic basis to ensure that these projects keep up to date with the other features being developed around them.

- Store your code in a centrally hosted location. In this book, we will be using GitHub, which is a free hosted service that allows all our code to be hosted in a central location to make sure that we do not need to be working on a specific laptop or have access to a specific server to be able to work on our code. If security is an issue, you can use a licensed version of GitHub to ensure that your code is private, or you can host a Git environment on your own servers to increase security even further.

- Allow your code to be reviewed by other developers. GitHub allows you to create requests to have your code reviewed by other developers and allow them to vote or approve the code changes made.

Using Git

If you want to collaborate with a few other developers, you will either need to have a Git server running or be using a Git hosting repository service. As we have mentioned earlier, we will be using GitHub as it is one of the most popular online repositories available to use and is free if you don't mind not being able to create private repositories.

Basic usage examples of Git

You can install Git directly on your PC or laptop and use it as a standalone application without any problems. As for our projects and examples, as well as having Git installed, we will set up an account with GitHub and create a new repository for storing all our apps that we develop for Splunk.

A lot of the work we will be doing with Git will be performed on the command line, but there is a little work to be done on the GitHub web interface. Git will also work with different **Integrated Development Environments (IDEs)**.

Create an account on GitHub

Let's start by creating an account on GitHub. Go to the following URL and create your own account: `https://github.com/`.

Take a little time to set up your account and add all your specific details and passwords. Make sure that you also set up SSH keys on GitHub as this will allow you to pull and push changes to and from the GitHub servers. You will still be able to create repositories and track and add changes, but you will not be able to make any of these changes public to other developers; they will only be available on the local PC or laptop you are developing on.

In the following example, we will work through setting up a repository to store an app.

Create your repository

Make sure you are happy with the free account as the repositories will be public. Within your account, you will have a **Repositories** tab; click on that and click on the **New** button. You will be presented with the following screen to give your repository a name and description and display it as **Public** or **Private**. When you are happy with the name, click on **Create Repository**:

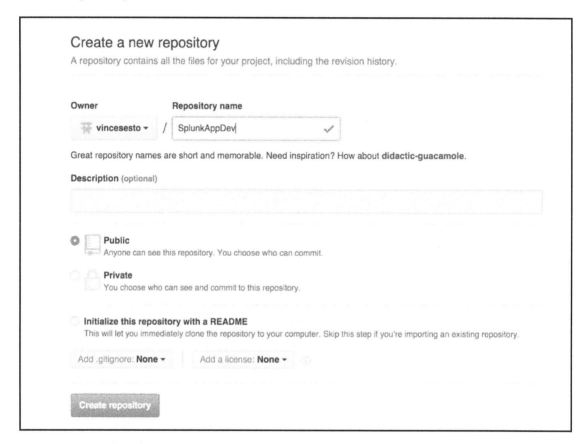

We are using the free version of GitHub. Please make sure you are happy with this before you start creating repositories that need to be kept private or have sensitive information. You may need to look at a different solution or pay for a Private GitHub repository.

For now, this means we have somewhere to store our repository, but we still need to initialize our repository where we will be developing it. We will create a simple README.md file in a development environment and initialize it:

1. Access your development environment and make sure it is set up to run Git.
2. Go to the directory that you want to be developing on.
3. Run the following command to create the README.md file and populate it with its first line:

```
echo "# SplunkAppDev" >> README.md
```

4. Then run the following Git command:

```
git init
```

5. We have now initialized our repository, which tells our Git installation that we are setting up a repository and everything inside this directory will be included. This now includes the new README.md file. We will be able to see that Git recognizes that we have initialized a repository, but does not know where to put the information. We will now see what Git is thinking about our code, add our README.md file, and then commit our changes to our repository in GitHub.

6. To see if there have been any changes made in your repository, run the status command:

```
git status
On branch master
Initial commit
Untracked files:
(use "git add <file>..." to include in what will be
committed)
README
nothing added to commit but untracked files present (use "git
add" to track)
```

7. We then use the add command to allow Git to track our new file:

```
git add .
```

8. When we are happy with all our additions, then we commit the changes that have been added:

```
git commit -m "Our first commit"
```

9. All this is still on our local Git application, so let GitHub know we are going to add some more information. Get the URL for the repository you have created and run the following command:

```
git remote add origin git@github.com:
<username>/<repository>.git
```

10. Finally, push your changes back to the remote repository on GitHub:

```
git push -u origin master
```

If you access the GitHub web interface again, you will be able to see the new files added to your repository.

Branching and working with Git

When we want to start working on development projects, creating features and bug fixes for application and code, the best thing we could do is create a branch from our master code. In our previous example, we simply added files and committed changes to our master branch. But what if we wanted to develop on one specific feature while someone else works on a bug in the code? This is where we can create a branch from our master branch of code and work on it in isolation, while our fellow developer creates a separate branch and works on their bug fix.

The best thing about branching is that we can use this to follow the development process that we outlined earlier in the chapter as we can create and develop on our branch, test these changes, before merging the code back into the master before we then deploy our changes to our test environment and then production.

The following diagram gives you a clear example of how the development branch is taken from our master code branch. Code is changed and commits are made to the code in which the new features are created. The changes are tested and once complete, a pull request is made, allowing other developers and our peers to view the changes and make sure there is nothing that we have missed or could have done in a more efficient way. Once the pull request is approved, we can merge our code branch into the master and deploy our changes into our production environment.

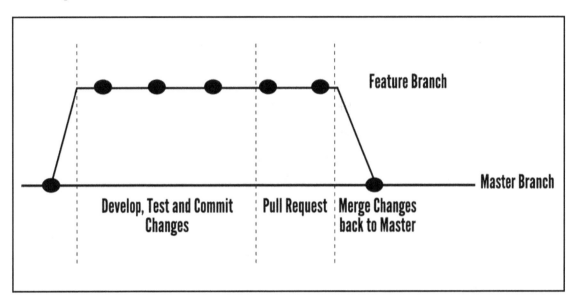

In the following example, we will create a branch from our master repository, make changes, and then merge the changes back into the master branch:

1. First we want to make sure that the master branch in the environment we are developing in is as up to date as possible, so we will be in sync with what is currently on GitHub:

   ```
   git pull
   ```

2. Then we use the checkout option to create a branch of our master code:

   ```
   git checkout -b branchname master
   ```

We then simply go about our work as we normally would, adding and committing changes as we did in our previous example and making sure we regularly push our changes back up to GitHub. Sometimes our development may run on for days and we should be merging changes from master back into our branch.

3. Move back to the master branch:

```
git checkout master
```

4. Grab any changes that have been made back onto our system:

```
git pull
```

5. Change back to our development branch:

```
git checkout branchname
```

6. Then merge any changes from the master back into our branch to make sure we are developing on the later version of code:

```
git merge master
```

So far, as part of our development process, we have been making changes to our code in a development branch, but at some point in time, we will want to be able to merge our branched code back into our master branch. Of course, this will only happen once we have successfully tested our changes in our development and test environment.

In these situations, it is simple to merge the branched code back into the master, but as we are working in a development team, we create a pull request, we ask that other developers to review our changes, and then once they are approved by our peers, they can be merged back into the master branch.

To create a pull request, we need to go back to our GitHub repository and click on the **New Pull Request** button at the top left of the screen. We will then be presented with a similar screen to the following one:

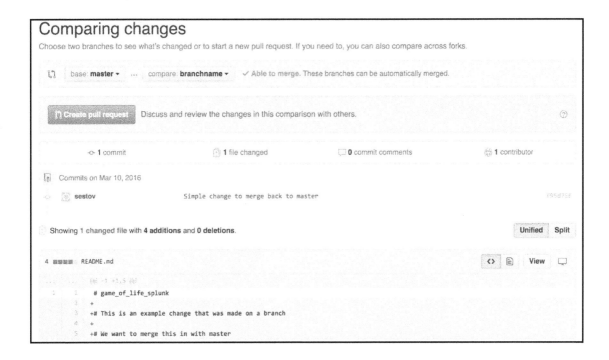

In the example screenshot, we can see that we are using the master branch as our base and using our branch (which in this case is called branchname) that we can compare it with. This feature of GitHub also shows us the differences between the two branches, where additions are in green, and if we removed code as part of our branch, we would see it highlighted in red. Once you then click on **Create Pull Request**, you are given the option to provide some more information about your changes, so your reviewers will then have some idea of what the code is doing. This is displayed in the following screenshot:

Once you create your `pull` request, you can then send the request out to other developers to allow them to view, comment on, and vote on your changes.

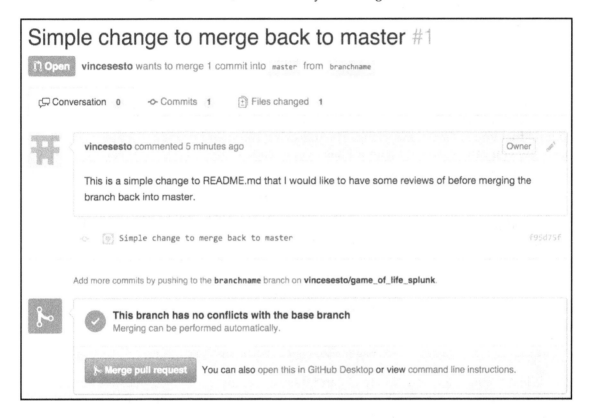

Once everyone is happy with the changes, click on the **Merge Pull Request** button at the bottom of the screen where your branch will be merged back into master, hopefully ready for your changes to be then deployed to your production environment.

Using Git when changes go bad

There may be some situations when a change has been implemented into production and testing within the development and test environments has missed some specific edge cases that are being hit when the code is released into production. This does happen occasionally, but when we are using Git, we have a way to quickly go back to our old release.

Within GitHub, you will be able to view a history of commits that have been made over the history of your development. Each commit is provided with a commit hash value, which is a 40-character alphanumeric value that can be used to then revert your changes to an earlier commit that you are sure is working. The following command uses an example commit hash, but you can locate your commit has to your code from GitHub. To revert changes, you can use the following command from the command line in your development environment:

```
git revert -r e088c3a4b62aec6729021945d6d2b0adc9734c72
```

The preceding command does not need to have the entire Git hash specified, but you can only provide the first five or so characters that provide enough information to identify the specific commit. The best thing about Git is that if ever a file system is corrupted, tampered with, or destroyed, we have the data stored and available on Git ready to be cloned back to our environment. In case of emergencies, the easiest thing that you might want to do is remove the directory that your application is located and then create a fresh clone of the data, as follows:

```
git clone git@github.com:username/repositoryname.git
```

This is just a simple introduction to Git and there are many books and websites that can give you a much more in-depth overview of using the application. It is definitely worth getting comfortable with applications such as Git if you are planning to continue working and developing in the technology sector.

Introducing the example projects

This is a good time to introduce the example projects that we are going to work on in the book. The three examples are varied in the type of data they are presenting, in the hope that the examples will present the user with different ways of visualizing and working with different data. It may be worth getting the data indexed so that you can start to get an idea of what we will be working with.

NASA HTTP data

Although the data is a little old, I think it can give an interesting insight into the web traffic for the NASAwebsite. The data is from 1995 and contains two traces of two months of all HTTP requests to the web server at the Kennedy Space Centre in Florida. The log files are Squid proxy logs and provide details on the host making the request, timestamp, request being made, HTTP reply code, and bytes in the reply.

A download of the data can be found at the following location: `http://ita.ee.lbl.gov/html/contrib/NASA-HTTP.html`.

```
199.72.81.55 - - [01/Jul/1995:00:00:01 -0400] "GET /history/apollo/ HTTP/1.0" 200 6245
unicomp6.unicomp.net - - [01/Jul/1995:00:00:06 -0400] "GET /shuttle/countdown/ HTTP/1.0" 200 3985
199.120.110.21 - - [01/Jul/1995:00:00:09 -0400] "GET /shuttle/missions/sts-73/mission-sts-73.html HTTP/1.0" 200 4085
burger.letters.com - - [01/Jul/1995:00:00:11 -0400] "GET /shuttle/countdown/liftoff.html HTTP/1.0" 304 0
199.120.110.21 - - [01/Jul/1995:00:00:11 -0400] "GET /shuttle/missions/sts-73/sts-73-patch-small.gif HTTP/1.0" 200 4179
burger.letters.com - - [01/Jul/1995:00:00:12 -0400] "GET /images/NASA-logosmall.gif HTTP/1.0" 304 0
burger.letters.com - - [01/Jul/1995:00:00:12 -0400] "GET /shuttle/countdown/video/livevideo.gif HTTP/1.0" 200 0
205.212.115.106 - - [01/Jul/1995:00:00:12 -0400] "GET /shuttle/countdown/countdown.html HTTP/1.0" 200 3985
d104.aa.net - - [01/Jul/1995:00:00:13 -0400] "GET /shuttle/countdown/ HTTP/1.0" 200 3985
129.94.144.152 - - [01/Jul/1995:00:00:13 -0400] "GET / HTTP/1.0" 200 7074
unicomp6.unicomp.net - - [01/Jul/1995:00:00:14 -0400] "GET /shuttle/countdown/count.gif HTTP/1.0" 200 40310
unicomp6.unicomp.net - - [01/Jul/1995:00:00:14 -0400] "GET /images/NASA-logosmall.gif HTTP/1.0" 200 786
unicomp6.unicomp.net - - [01/Jul/1995:00:00:14 -0400] "GET /images/KSC-logosmall.gif HTTP/1.0" 200 1204
d104.aa.net - - [01/Jul/1995:00:00:15 -0400] "GET /shuttle/countdown/count.gif HTTP/1.0" 200 40310
d104.aa.net - - [01/Jul/1995:00:00:15 -0400] "GET /images/NASA-logosmall.gif HTTP/1.0" 200 786
d104.aa.net - - [01/Jul/1995:00:00:15 -0400] "GET /images/KSC-logosmall.gif HTTP/1.0" 200 1204
129.94.144.152 - - [01/Jul/1995:00:00:17 -0400] "GET /images/ksclogo-medium.gif HTTP/1.0" 304 0
199.120.110.21 - - [01/Jul/1995:00:00:17 -0400] "GET /images/launch-logo.gif HTTP/1.0" 200 1713
```

The example projects will help analyze the web traffic hitting the NASA website and provide visualization and insights into the site's usage. The data will allow us to start with basic visualizations within the SplunkWeb Framework.

Game of life

If you have been working in development, even for a short period of time, I am sure you will have heard of *Conway's Game of Life*. Even though it's called a game, it's more of a simulation of biological cells, where we can watch the cells evolve to either live or fail. The cells are governed by a set of rules that determines if they live or die through each generation or step in the simulation:

1. Any live cell with fewer than two live neighbors will die, as if caused by under-population.
2. Any live cell with two or three live neighbors lives on to the next generation.
3. Any live cell with more than three live neighbors dies, as if caused by overpopulation.
4. Any dead cell with exactly three live neighbors becomes a live cell, as if caused by reproduction.

The logs presented here are random, but will consist of the grid where the cells will live, a timestamp, and the cells that are present through each generation of the life cycle (`https://en.wikipedia.org/wiki/Conway%27s_Game_of_Life`).

I have created a GitHub repository with a basic example of *Conway's Game Of Life*, but I have also produced logs for the script for 2 hours to give you some sample data that can be worked with through the examples. The sample Python script and log file can be found by going to the following link: `https://github.com/vincesesto/game_of_life_splunk`.

From here, you can index the file called `game_of_life.log`. If you are using at least version 6 of Splunk, the logs will be indexed correctly with the events separated correctly for each date and timestamp. The sample log file will look similar to the following image:

```
2016-03-09 03:44:57
Game of Life -- Generation 1
# # # # # # # # # # # # # # # # # # # #

#                   G              G        G #

#                       G     G    G     G G #

#    G       G             G        G G       #

# # # # # # # # # # # # # # # # # # # #


2016-03-09 03:44:58
Game of Life -- Generation 2
# # # # # # # # # # # # # # # # # # # #

#                               G     G G G #

#                               G     G G #

#                             G G G G       #

# # # # # # # # # # # # # # # # # # # #


2016-03-09 03:45:00
Game of Life -- Generation 3
# # # # # # # # # # # # # # # # # # # #

#                             G G     G #

#                                           #

#                             G G     G G #

# # # # # # # # # # # # # # # # # # # #
```

The example data that we have will allow us to analyze the simulation of cells, and although the data is not very complex, we should hopefully provide some interesting visualizations and take our skills with the Splunk Web Framework further.

Historical stock market data

Yahoo! Finance provides an API that allows people to download historical stock market data directly to their environment. In our example, we will take a few different companies and download their historical data for the year 2015, displaying the date stamp, opening value for the day, highest value of the day, lowest value for the day, closing value, volume traded for the day, and adjusted close value of the stock. The sample data will be in CSV form and the API call will be similar to the following URL: .

The API call is pretty straightforward and the commands are listed here:

- s: Company symbol (Yahoo!)
- d: To month −1
- e: To day
- f: To year
- g: Set up of date (d for day, m for month, y for yearly)
- a: From month -1
- b: From day (two digits)
- c: From year

For more details on different company symbols and more explanations of the data that the API can provide, go to the Yahoo! Finance site at `https://finance.yahoo.com/`.

```
Date,Open,High,Low,Close,Volume,Adj Close
2010-01-28,15.93,15.96,15.44,15.44,30159500,15.44
2010-01-27,16.459999,16.49,15.77,15.98,41701000,15.98
2010-01-26,15.82,16.17,15.70,15.99,43979400,15.99
2010-01-25,16.07,16.110001,15.74,15.86,19683700,15.86
2010-01-22,16.08,16.209999,15.81,15.88,25132800,15.88
2010-01-21,16.389999,16.58,16.10,16.200001,21858400,16.200001
2010-01-20,16.65,16.68,16.25,16.379999,14419500,16.379999
2010-01-19,16.780001,16.959999,16.639999,16.75,15182600,16.75
2010-01-15,17.25,17.25,16.75,16.82,18415000,16.82
2010-01-14,16.809999,17.23,16.799999,17.120001,16715600,17.120001
2010-01-13,16.879999,16.98,16.65,16.90,16955600,16.90
2010-01-12,16.65,16.860001,16.60,16.68,15672400,16.68
2010-01-11,16.77,16.83,16.48,16.74,16181900,16.74
2010-01-08,16.68,16.76,16.620001,16.700001,15470000,16.700001
2010-01-07,16.809999,16.90,16.57,16.700001,31816300,16.700001
```

The data presented is an interesting sample is varied, allowing for interesting trend analysis. This is where we will take our skills further and start to use more of the advanced features of the Splunk Web Framework.

Summary

In this chapter, we covered the fundamentals of the Splunk Web Framework, including the architecture of the environment and an explanation of all the different components. We have walked through the development process and discussed having a good procedure in place before you start to develop. We took a look at Git, the application and hosting code repositories on GitHub, and finally the example data we are going to be working on through the rest of the book.

We also outlined some of the reasons behind the book and the hope that we will be able to bring you on an interesting and motivating journey into the Splunk Web Framework.

It feels like we have been doing a lot of reading and not a lot of work, but hold on! The next chapter is going take is into the work of Splunk App creation using the Splunk Web Framework. We will get our feet wet with our first Splunk App using the Web Interface; we will create dashboards and basic dashboard elements for our App. We will also gain an understanding of the structure of Splunk Apps and their file structure and discuss why it is important to understand our audience.

2
Presenting Data to Users as a Splunk App

This book assumes that you have already used Splunk in the past and are familiar with searching and administration of the application. So by now you have most likely seen how Splunk is able to visualize your searches into graphs and reports. Although Splunk indexing and searching is a major aspect of the application, the visualization is where Splunk takes things to the next level as it means that you can save reports and tailor graphs to allow non-Splunk users to simply access and see the results they need without having to know the inner workings of how the data is transferred to Splunk and how the search requests are constructed.

In this chapter, we will continue to develop our knowledge of the Splunk Web Framework and learn the following:

- What Splunk Apps are and why is it important for us to use them
- How to create Splunk App from the web interface and the command line
- The basic Splunk App file structure
- Creating dashboards and panels within our Splunk App and starting to create visualizations of our data
- How to create and design tools that are catered specifically to your user
- Further our working knowledge of Git

A Splunk app is the first part in controlling your visual interface and segregating relevant data into a logical area that users will know has the data and reports that they need. A Splunk app also allows developers to more closely follow a development process as discussed in the previous chapter as your development will be centered around a specific aspect of an app, segregated away from the rest of Splunk, where development and testing can continue uninterrupted.

If you want to break things down into its simplest terms, a Splunk app is a container. The following diagram gives a rough idea of a Splunk app in this mindset, with a bottle as our container with many dashboards, charts, and visualizations. You may have one dashboard or report, or you may have many. Ultimately, you could simply have a Splunk app that has nothing inside it. The main search interface of Splunk is, in itself, a Splunk app.

 Is a Splunk Add-on the same as a Splunk app? The simple answer is no. A Splunk Add-on is similar to a Splunk app as it is a stand alone piece of code that is installed on your system in a similar way to a Splunk app, but instead it provides different functionality. A Splunk Add-on runs on the platform but provides a specific capability to other Splunkapps, such gathering or collecting data or processing it or mapping extra data and usually does not run as a standalone application. In this book, as we are focusing on the visual aspects of Splunk we will not be doing any specific work on create Splunk Add-on's. For more information on the difference between an app and an Add-on, please refer to the Splunk developers guide at the following URL:
`http://dev.splunk.com/view/dev-guide/SP-CAAAE28.`

Just before we move a little further, I just want to make sure we are clear about some definitions about the explanation of a Splunk app. We stated that a Splunk app is a container for dashboards. A Dashboard is a collection of panels grouped together to provide a user interface to the user. Panels are individual items including graphs, charts, or visualization items that present a single set of information within the dashboard. This is usually in the form of a saved search or the result of a report.

Managing and creating your apps

When we first log on to Splunk, we are presented with the home page, which provides us with a list of all our appsdown the left-hand side of the screen and we are able to order it to our liking. By clicking on the Splunk logo at the top left of the screen, we are brought to the home page `http://localhost:8000/en-GB/app/launcher/home`.

The following screenshot shows the welcome page that is presented when the user logs on to Splunk. The left panel running down the side of the screen allows you to drag and order the Splunk apps, allowing you to place the most important apps up the top of the screen ready for you to use. Above the list of Splunkapps, you will also see the icon of a cog, next to the word **Apps.** By clicking on this icon you are taken to the **Manage Apps** screen.

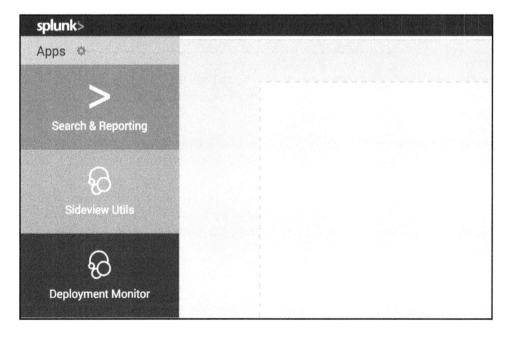

If you are not on the main home screen in Splunk, you can also access the **Manage Apps** screen by clicking on the **Apps** menu, which is positioned in the top left-hand corner, next to the Splunk icon. If you are an **Administrator** of a Splunk environment, you may have made use of the interface that Splunkprovides to allow you to manage, configure, and create your apps.

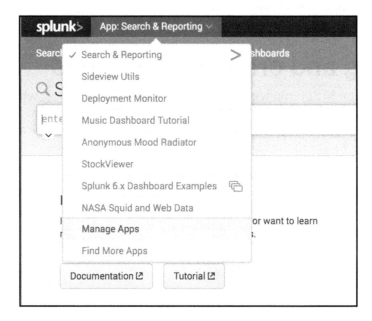

The **Manage Apps** configuration page allows you to see all of the Splunk apps within your current environment and allows you to perform a number of different tasks to manage your Splunk apps, including the following:

- **Search for prebuilt apps**: Access the Splunk base to search, download, and install prebuilt and approved Splunk apps and Add-ons. Refer to `https://splunkbase.splunk.com/`.

- **Install a Splunk app from a file**: Not just Splunk apps and Add-ons from the Splunk base, but any packaged Splunk app that you or someone else may have created and are ready to deploy in your environment can be installed.

- **Enable and disable Splunk apps**: Any Splunk app that is currently installed in your environment can be enabled or disabled at any time. There is no way to delete a Splunkapp from the **Management** console, but this can be achieved from the command line, and we will discuss this later in the chapter.
- **Manage permissions of your Splunk apps**: Change and configure which users can access and make changes to any of the Splunk apps installed on your environment. You can also change whether or not it is visible to users.
- **Configure your Splunk apps**: Make adjustments to the configurations that your Splunk app utilizes and change the specific objects the Splunk app has access to.
- **Create new Splunk apps**: This is what we will do next.

Creating our first Splunk app

We are going to discuss designing applications later in the chapter, but for now it's time to get stuck in our first example Splunk app using our NASA website data. For now, we are going to create the most basic Splunk app to get things started. To create our first application, you can use the following process:

1. As shown in the following screenshot, go to the top of the screen and click on the **Create App** button:

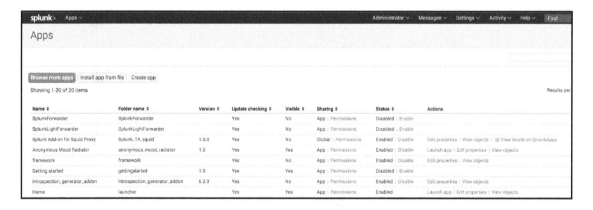

2. You will then be presented with the following page, asking for the details of the Splunk app that you are going to create:

3. Use the following details to fill in this form:
    - **Name**: This is the text presented on the Splunk web interface as the app. Our new app will be called `NASA Squid and Web Data`.
    - **Folder name**: This is the name of the directory that will be created on the server and can be accessed via the command line. Enter the folder name of `nasa_squid_web_data`.
    - **Version**: As our first iteration of our new Splunk app, we enter the value `0.1`.
    - **Visible**: This is if you want to make your new Splunk app visible from the point of creation. In this instance, it is **Yes**.
    - **Author**: This is the person who is developing the Splunk app, so enter your name.
    - **Description**: Provide a brief description of the Splunk app you are creating.
    - **Template**: This is the type of Splunk app that you want to create. At this point in time, we only have a **barebones** or a **Simple** template. In this instance, we will use the **barebones** template. In later chapters, we will create our own template from existing Splunkapps to create some consistency across our development.
    - **Upload asset**: Please leave this blank, but if you need to ever load static images, scripts, or CSS that your Splunk App uses, this is where you put it.
4. Then click on the **Save** button at the bottom of the screen to complete the Splunk App creation.

That's it! You have created your first Splunk app. You will see the new Splunk app listed in the **Manage Apps** screen. You will also be able to see the new Splunk app listed on the left-hand side of the home screen. By clicking on the **NASA Squid and Web Data** app, you will be taken to your new Splunk app. And from what you can see, it looks similar to the original **Search and Reporting** screen, with the basic Splunk search bar, and a basic menu, including **Search**, **Pivot**, **Reports**, **Alerts**, and **Dashboards**.

It might feel like we still have not come very far, but we are laying the groundwork to ramp things up shortly.

Alternative ways to create a Splunk app

You don't always have to use the web interface to create your Splunk apps. There are two other ways by which we can create our Splunk apps: with a Splunk command on the server or by creating the basic directory structure.

To create a Splunk app from the command line, first access the Splunk server and run the following command:

```
$SPLUNK_HOME/bin/splunk create app splunk_app_name -template template_name
```

Here is the description of the preceding command:

- `$SPLUNK_HOME`: This is the location of your Splunk installation on your server.
- `splunk_app_name`: This will be the name of the Splunk app you want to create. As you may remember, in our example, we named our Splunk app `NASA Squid and Web Data`.
- `template_name`: This will be either `barebones` or `sample_app`.

When you are accessing the command line of your server, you will be able to see the location of all the Splunk apps on your environment. The location is as follows:

`$SPLUNK_HOME/etc/apps`

Looking through the directory, you should be able to see all your environment Splunk apps, including the new one you have just created; in this instance, it should be the same name as the folder name you provided in the **Create Apps** form as `nasa_squid_web_data`. Although we advise against creating a Splunkapp straight from the filesystem, the specific files that you need to create to create a new Splunk app are listed as follows:

- `$SPLUNK_HOME/etc/apps/splunk_app_name/default/app.conf`
- `$SPLUNK_HOME/etc/apps/splunk_app_name/local`
- `$SPLUNK_HOME/etc/apps/splunk_app_name/metadata/default.meta`
- `$SPLUNK_HOME/etc/apps/splunk_app_name/default/data/ui/views/`

You need to have your XML data files in the views directory, and we will be working on these files in the next chapter.

Adding your new Splunk app to Git

In some situations, you may want to create one repository for all Splunk apps, but I always recommend that you have one repository for each of your Splunk apps. Although it may be annoying in a case where you are trying to recover a deleted directory because you may have numerous Splunk apps to retrieve, it will be a lot more efficient when you are updating or releasing Splunk apps on your environment. You will only need to deploy or update one Splunk app instead of the entire set of Splunk apps you have in your environment. To create a new repository for our new NASA data and add our Splunk app to the repository, we perform the following steps:

1. Create the repository with the name `nasa_squid_web_data` and use the description `NASA Squid and Web Data Splunk App`.
2. Log on to your Splunk server and change to the directory of the new app you have created:

   `cd $SPLUNK_HOME/etc/apps/nasa_squid_web_data`

3. Initialize the new repository with all the current files in there:

```
git init
```

5. Add all the content to the repository with a full stop (.):

```
git add .
```

6. Commit all your changes to the repository:

```
git commit -m "Our first Splunk App Commit"
```

7. Set up the remote location of your repository:

```
git remote add origin git@github.com:
<account>/nasa_squid_web_data.git
```

8. Now push all your changes back to GitHub:

```
git push -u origin master
```

Deleting Splunk apps

If there is ever a situation in which you would like to completely delete a Splunk app from your environment, the only way you can do this is by deleting the directory from the filesystem on your Splunk server. With our new **NASA Web Data App**, we can delete it with the following command:

```
rm -rf $SPLUNK_HOME/etc/apps/nasa_squid_web_data
```

To activate this change, you will also need to restart the Splunk server. The awesome thing is that if you happened to make this change by accident and had a repository set up in GitHub, all you would need to do to restore this Splunk app is log on to the Splunk server and run the following Git command from the command line:

```
git clone git@github.com:<account>/nasa_squid_web_data.git
$SPLUNK_HOME/etc/apps
```

The Splunk app directory structure

Now that we are on our Splunk server, it is a good time to run through the different files and directories in our Splunk apps.

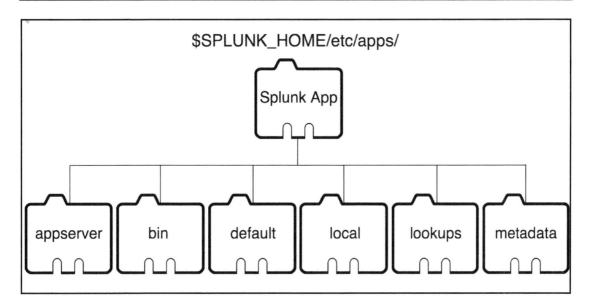

As we stated earlier in the chapter, there are four basic directories and files that need to be set up for you to have a Splunk app. The following is a more detailed list of the directory structure and files included.

- **appserver**: The appserver directory includes some of the files that are used as part of the inner workings of your Splunk app. Within this directory, you will see the static directory that will include your CSS, JavaScript, and other files required to configure your app.
- **bin**: The bin directory, as with normal server directory structures, contains binary files, including shell scripts and Python scripts used in delivering your Splunk apps.
- **default**: When you eventually publish your Splunk app ready for production, all your configuration, search, and display data will be moved into the default directory. You will notice that when you make changes to your Splunk apps through the web interface, the changes will be added to the local directory, leaving the default directory pristine.
- **local**: As we stated earlier, any changes that are made to searches, views, or other configurations by the local user are added to the local directory.
- **lookups**: These lookups are specific to your Splunk app searches, which will use CSV files to enhance the data that you currently have indexed in Splunk.
- **metadata**: All objects that are used in Splunk have permissions, and the metadata file includes all the permissions for these objects.

Designing Splunk apps for your audience

When creating your Splunk apps, the first thing you need to realize is that you need to understand the audience that you are creating an app for, so that you can specifically meet their needs. We can do amazing things with the Splunk Web Framework, but the apps you create will only be valuable if someone is actually using them or consuming information.

When it comes to designing Splunk apps, I like to brainstorm as many ideas as possible, as the best thing about the Splunk Web Framework is that you can rapidly prototype ideas. Also, when it comes to designing Splunk apps, I like to work with the four **D**s to **Discover**, **Define**, **Develop**, and **Deliver**. This process is used to help try and think of multiple ideas, try to expand as many ideas as possible, and relate these ideas back to what your user needs. Then try to narrow the focus of the ideas and prioritize what you think is the best thing to deliver.

When we use the four Ds, we:

- **Discover**: This is where we discuss what the user actually needs and try and gather as many different ideas that specifically address this.
- **Define**: This is where we try to define the business objectives with what we are designing and try to align them with what the user actually needs.
- **Develop**: This is where we get to create and develop different solutions to what the user needs, in iterative stages, and test the functionality of what we are creating.
- **Deliver**: The is the final iterative delivery of the application, where we provide further testing in the production environment and gather feedback from the user and the business to further enhance what we have provided.

We can use the four Ds to do a simple exercise with our example of the NASA Squid and Web Data Splunk app. We should have probably done this before we even created our basic Splunk app, but we at least knew that we needed to make this Splunk app. We can also make a number of assumptions with our design process to allow us to move forward, but in real life, you should be able to go directly to your users to gather initial information. If we follow the four Ds once again for our example, we can see the following:

- **Discover**: The user needs to see the squid and web data in a visual format. We will have both technical and non-technical users, and in this instance, we will only create one Splunk app for both of these users. We can also assume that not all our technical users will be comfortable working with Splunk, Splunk searches, and reports. In this part of the process, we would start to brainstorm on how we can set up our interface to present the information to the user.

- **Define**: As the data that we have for our NASA website is specifically squid logs, we will make some assumptions that our non-technical users are more interested in seeing traffic and popularity of certain pages, whereas the more technical users will want information related to errors, throughput, and return codes from the web server. At this point, we would want to brainstorm as many ideas as possible and try to get them all down on paper, as thinking differently can sometimes give us some more interesting ideas. The following section has a drawing of our first dashboard, which will provide details on the following:
    - Return codes from the web server
    - The top 10 popular pages being accessed
    - The average hits per day
- **Develop**: This is the fun part, and we are going to kick off our development shortly to complete our first iteration of our Splunk app.
- **Deliver**: This will be when we communicate the release of our Splunk app with our users, perform training on how to use it, and ask for feedback.

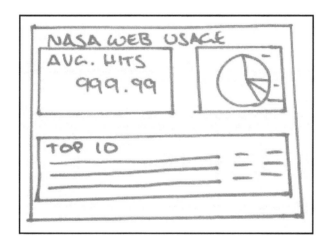

As you can see in the preceding diagram, your initial hand-drawn designs do not need to be perfect but only need to convey the idea you are trying to get across. The idea you choose to develop will then be taken forward and worked on.

Creating a dashboard

It's now time to add some useful interface dashboards and panels to our new Splunk app. So we open our NASA Squid and Web Data Splunk App, and click on the dashboard menu at the top of the screen to get things started:

1. At the top-right side of the page, you will see the Create New Dashboard button. Click on the button and you will be presented with the following form:

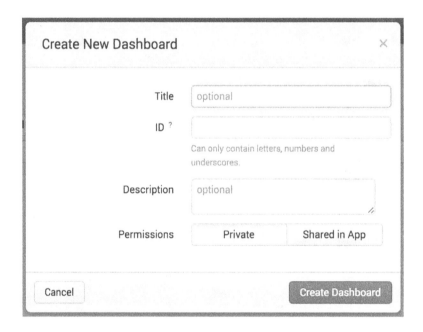

2. Fill in the form with the following details:
   - **Title:** NASA Web Usage
   - **Description:** Summary page for our new Splunk Dashboard
   - **Permissions: Shared in App**
3. Then click on the **Create Dashboard** button.

You have created an empty dashboard, which should like what is shown in the following screenshot. The dashboard is already in **Edit** mode, allowing us to continue to use the web interface to create panels to display the sets of data that we discussed in the design phase.

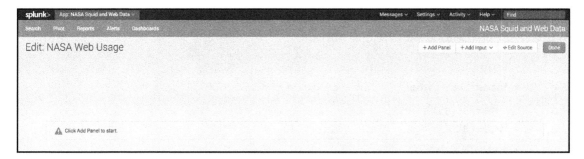

Within the page, you can see we have three buttons that we can use to control how we edit the dashboard that we have created for our Splunk app:

- **Add Panel**: This allows us to add a new or existing panel that has been shared across our environment. If we had a large existing environment, we would be able to search for any of the visualizations that have been shared across our different Splunk apps.
- **Add Input**: This allows our users to interact with our dashboard and assist them to customize the information that is presented to the user. We will be covering this in later chapters.
- **Edit Source**: This allows us to directly configure and script the SimpleXML code that underlies our Splunk web interface. This will be covered in later chapters as well.

Field extraction for our NASA data

Before we set up our new panels, we need to set up some field extraction to allow us to simplify our Splunk searches that we use. We are not using advanced searches within our examples as we are focusing more on the Splunk web framework, but this will allow our searches to be more efficient as we only need to search for a field instead of adding extra parameters to our search.

The following is a breakdown of the field extraction we are using with an example output. From the squid log event:

```
home100.nj.nec.com - - [27/Jul/1995:23:59:59 -0400] "GET /images/WORLD-
logosmall.gif HTTP/1.0" 200 669
```

We have set up the following field extraction:

- **From**: home100.nj.nec.com
- **SquidDateTime**: [27/Jul/1995:23:59:59 -0400]
- **RequestType**: GET
- **Request**: /images/WORLD-logosmall.gif
- **ReturnCode**: 200
- **ReturnSize**: 669

The specific regex we have used as our field extraction is listed as follows:

```
^(?P<From>[^ ]+)\s+\-\s+\-
\s+(?P<SquidDateTime>\[\d+/\w+/\d+:\d+:\d+:\d+\s+\-\d+\])[^ \n]*
"(?P<RequestType>\w+)\s+(?P<Request>[^
]+)[^"\n]*"\s+(?P<ReturnCode>\d+)\s+(?P<ReturnSize>\d+)
```

Finally, to set up an average of values per month, we have also extracted the day for the month with a second field extraction. Using the preceding example: MonthDay: 27, the specific regex we have used as our field extraction is listed as follows:

```
^(?:[^\-\n]*\-){2}\s+\[(?P<MonthDay>\d+)
```

If you are having trouble with the field extraction, we have included this in the example code that can be downloaded as part of this chapter. The field extraction will be set up as part of the props.conf file in the default directory.

Adding panels to our dashboard

Let's start by setting up a pie chart that will display our return codes from our squid logs for the NASA website. If you are no longer in the edit screen for the NASA Web Usage dashboard, click on the **Dashboard** menu of your Splunk app, click on **Edit Action**, and select **Edit Panel:**

1. Click on the **Add Panel** button, select **New**, and click on the **Pie** option. You will then be presented with the following form:

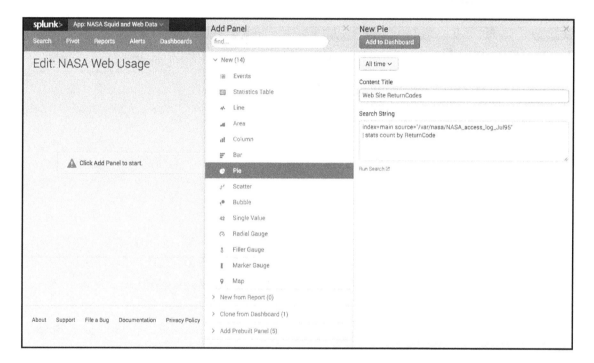

2. For the form, set the following values:
   - Set the time range to **All Time**
   - Give the panel a title, such as `Web Site ReturnCode`

3. Add the search string that Splunk will use to create your visualization. In this instance, we are going to use the following search:

```
index=main sourcetype=NASASquidLogs
| stats count by ReturnCode
```

4. Click on the **Add** to **Dashboard** button.

5. Then click on the **Done** button, and you will have your new panel added to your dashboard:

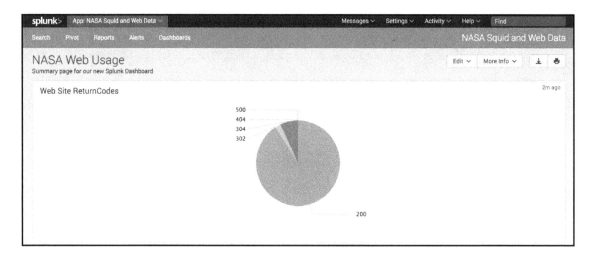

Let's keep going and add a **Single Value** panel to display the average hits to the website per day:

1. Get into the **Edit** screen again for our dashboard. If you still have the preceding screen, displaying the new pie chart, you would have noticed by now that there is an **Edit** button directly on the dashboard.
2. Click on the **Edit** button and select **Edit Panel**.

3. To add a **Single Value** panel, click on **Add Panel** and select **New**.

4. From the list, select **Single Value**.

5. When you are presented with the form to add your new panel, enter the following information:
   - Set the time range to **All Time**
   - Add **Content Title** as Average Hits Per Day

6. Add the new search to be used for the **Single Value** panel as follows:

```
index=main sourcetype=NASASquidLogs
| stats count by MonthDay
| stats avg(count) AS AvgHitsPerDay
```

7. Click on **Add to Dashboard**.

8. Finally, we want to add a **Statistics Table** to our dashboard to display the top 10 requested items within the squid logs.

9. You should still be in edit panel mode, but if you are not, click on the **Edit** button and select **Edit Panel**.

10. Click on **Add Panel**, select **New**, and select **Statistics Panel** from the list.

11. Set **Content Title** as **Top 10 Website Requests.**

12. Add the new Splunk search that will be used for the table to the following values:

```
index=main sourcetype=NASASquidLogs
| top 10 Request
```

13. Click on **Add to Dashboard**.

14. As you have created all the visualizations for our iterations, click on the **Done** button.

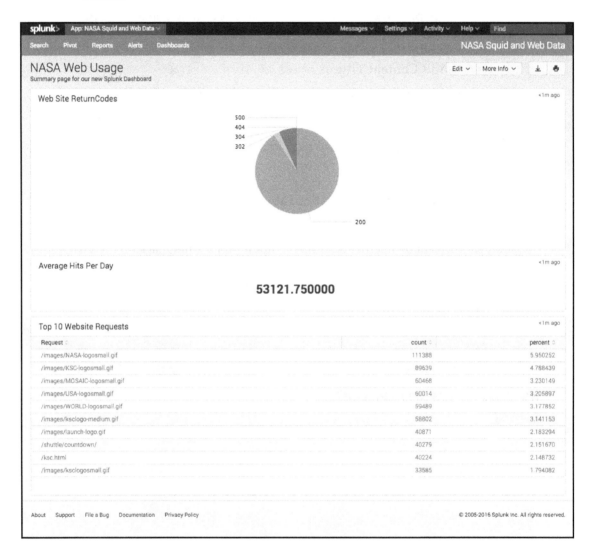

So, we're done. The first iteration of our new Splunk app has all the panels and functionality added, but it doesn't really look the way we wanted it to look when we drew our rough sketch during the design phase. There seems to be a lot of wasted space and I think we can make things a little nicer.

Editing existing dashboards

We have created all of the data visualizations and panels for our first iteration of our NASA Squid and Web Data Splunk App, but we want to make the interface a little clearer to the user. We have used the edit feature previously to add extra panels, but in this instance, we will make some changes to the way the dashboard displays. Again, click on the **Edit** button in the top right of the dashboard screen and select **Edit Panels**.

When you select **Edit Panel**, you will notice that you are still presented with the graph or chart as you would normally see it in the dashboard, but you have a number of extra options available on the web interface. The top right of each of the panels gives you full editing control of the panel with the following features:

- The *X* and grey line beside it allow you to quickly delete or reposition the panel around your dashboard
- The cog allows you to rename the panel, delete it, or convert it to a prebuilt panel to speed up searches
- The magnifying glass lets you change the name of the panel and reconfigure aspects of the Splunksearch being used
- The smaller chart image allows you to change the type of visualisation being used
- The paint brush then refers to the way that your visualization is presented on the dashboard

With our new dashboard, we want to have *Average Hits Per Day* and *Web Site ReturnCodes* displayed next to each other:

1. To make this change, position your mouse pointer on the grey line at the top of the **Web Site ReturnCodes** panel, and it will turn into a four-pointed cross.
2. When you hold your mouse button down, you will see that you can drag the panel around the screen.
3. Move the panel to the right-hand side of the **Average Hits Per Day** panel.
4. The web interface will then rearrange your panels to allow them to fit next to each other.
5. We now want to change our **Average Hits Per Day Single Value** panel, to have our search result only provide two decimal places, and add a label underneath the value.
6. Click on the magnifying glass for the **Single Value** panel and select **Edit Search String**.

7. Add the following line to the end of your search string:

```
| eval AvgHitsPerDay=round(AvgHitsPerDay,2)
```

8. Then click on the paint brush icon and add *Hits Per Day* as an **Under Label**.

9. Click on the **Done** button. Your changes will be saved and your dashboard should look like the following screenshot:

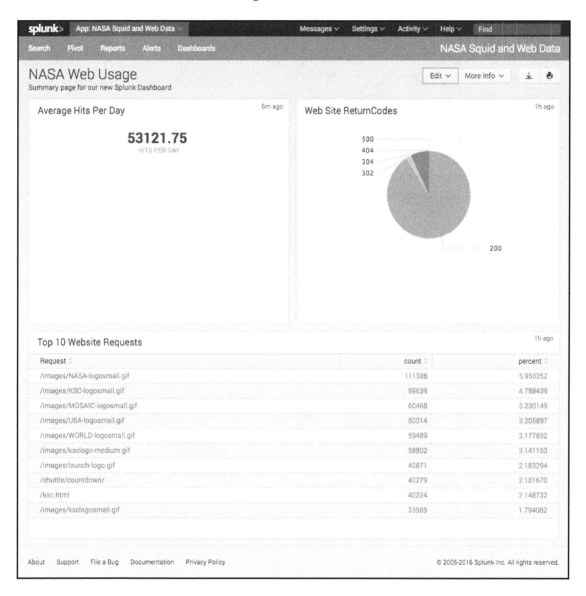

In a small amount of time, I think your users will be pretty impressed with the dashboard we have set up for them, handing over the first iteration of our Splunk app. We have been able to create a functional dashboard that gives useful insights into what their data is providing. At this point in time, there is no way to use the web interface to change what page or dashboard is provided by default for our Splunk app. We will show you in later chapters how to use SimpleXML code to configure the page that is displayed by default to the user when they open the Splunk app. We can, however, display our dashboard in the Splunkhome screen and we will make this change next.

Set your dashboard on the Splunk home screen

Whenever we want to return to our home page in Splunk, unless we have previously changed the default page being displayed, it will provide a blank page as we saw earlier in this chapter. Setting our new NASA Web Usage dashboard as the default dashboard on our home screen can be achieved with the following steps:

1. For the NASA Web Usage dashboard, click on the **Edit** option and select **Set as Home Dashboard**.
2. Click on the **Dashboards** menu at the top of the Splunk app.
3. Access the NASA squid and Web Data Splunk App.

4. So, every time your users go to the home page, your new dashboard that you have created will be displayed: `http://localhost:8000/en-GB/app/launcher/home`.

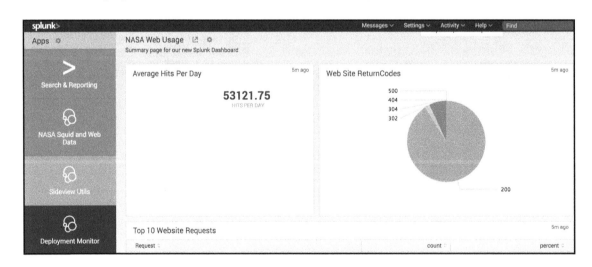

Viewing and saving changes to GitHub

We've now made a few changes to our Splunk app and this should be added to our repository. We can view changes made by running the Git `status` command from the command line. We can also see a log of all the changes we have made with the Git log command. So, to view the changes we have made and to add our new dashboard to our repository, we perform the following steps:

1. Log on to the Splunk server and change to your Splunk app directory:

   ```
   cd $SPLUNK_HOME/etc/apps/nasa_squid_web/
   ```

2. Check the status of your current filesystem in relation to Git:

   ```
   git status
   On branch master
   Your branch is up-to-date with 'origin/master'.
   Untracked files:
   (use "git add <file>..." to include in what will be
   committed)
   local/data/
   nothing added to commit but untracked files present (use "git
   add" to track)
   ```

3. You will notice that the local/data directory is not currently being tracked. To add this to your repository, use the add command as we did previously:

   ```
   git add .
   ```

4. Now commit the changes to your repository:

   ```
   git commit -m "Adding our first dashboard"
   ```

5. Finally, push the changes back to GitHub:

   ```
   git push -u origin master
   ```

So far, we are using the master branch, which does not really follow our development process. In our next chapter, we will start to create branches of our repository so that we can start to allow development work to continue across multiple branches without affecting our master code.

Summary

In this chapter, you were introduced to Splunk apps, why it's important to make use of them, and the basic server file structure of a Splunk app. We started to make use of the Splunk Web Framework, utilizing the web interface to create our first Splunk app. We also created a dashboard for our app and added panels representing different visualizations of the NASA Squid Web Logs.

We then used the web interface to edit existing panels and dashboard configurations. We also looked at the design so that we can specifically try to address the needs of our users and the business. Our work with Git has also been furthered as we were able to create a new repository for our Splunk app and commit further changes from our environment.

In the next chapter, we will move further into the Splunk Web Framework as we dive into Simple XML, with a discussion of the code and a breakdown of how to take our Splunk apps further by developing with Simple XML. We will start to work with the Splunk code editor, and start to learn some of the more advanced features of the dashboard and panel elements.

As we continue to work with Splunk, we will continue to use Git to track our changes and modifications to our code, and we will start separating our code into branches to segregate feature releases and ensure that they are not affecting our master code.

3
Expand Your Splunk Apps Using Simple XML

By now, you have started to learn that the Splunk Web Framework allows you to make attractive and functional dashboards with ease through the web interface. You may be wondering why we would want to complicate things by diverging from this and using code to configure and manipulate our Splunk apps and interface. Well, the web interface has come a long way in the past few years and you can achieve quite a lot, but there are still some things that you cannot do and need to turn to the code to achieve them.

This is where SimpleXML comes in. As we saw at the end of our last chapter, we were not able to change the default display page of our Splunk app using the web interface. This and many other things can be achieved by attacking the Splunk SimpleXML code directly. SimpleXML is the underlying code to your dashboards and panels that you have created so far using the Splunk web interface. In this chapter, you will also begin to see that due to the simplicity of SimpleXML, with little practice, you will be able to develop your Splunk app faster than by using the web interface.

In this chapter, we will continue to develop our knowledge of the Splunk Web Framework and learn the following:

- We will provide an introduction to SimpleXML and expand our example application further by using SimpleXML instead of the web interface
- How to change and manipulate your code using the Splunk code editor
- Use SimpleXML to create our visualizations and charts on our dashboards
- Continue to look at the file structure of Splunk and discuss how file precedence and Splunk web caching can interfere with our code development
- We will further our knowledge of the development process by creating a development branch of our repository in Git

Unlike other development languages, the code is simple and straightforward as it is based on **Extensible Markup Language** (**XML**), which basically defines a set of rules for encoding your document in a format that is both human readable and machine readable. Within this chapter, we will start to explore the SimpleXML rules and definitions that allow us to continue to expand the Splunk Web Framework. SimpleXML was a basic XML language with its main function to get users familiar with the Splunk code editor and eventually allow them to move on to working with advanced XML. This is no longer the case as we discussed in the first chapter, as advanced XML is being deprecated, with functionality being added to SimpleXML to make sure that it is no longer the poorer cousin of advanced XML.

File precedence and caching

The syntax of SimpleXML is not overly complex but needs to be adhered to so that your pages work as they are supposed to. If you have worked with other scripting languages, you may notice that if you leave out an ending tag or misspell a specific tag, the item will not be displayed or may be displayed incorrectly. If you make a mistake with SimpleXML, when you reload the page, you may be presented with the following page, which once again brings us back to ensuring that we have an appropriate development process so that we limit the chances of a page like that being presented to the end user:

---

400 Bad Request

Return to Splunk home page

XML Syntax Error: expected '>', line 66, column 1

View more information about your request (request ID = 56fdded72c1164e5750) in Search

You are logged into **localhost:8000** as **admin**, which is connected to splunkd @**264376** at **https://127.0.0.1:8089** on **Fri Apr 1 13:37:11 2016**.

Before we move forward in using SimpleXML, we will touch on the precedence that Splunk uses to look through files and how it caches data. This may be useful when developing with the Splunk Web Framework as you may be making a change to a Splunk app, but the change will not take effect on the Splunk web interface. As we discussed in the previous chapter, there is a default and local folder in your Splunk apps. These folders are set up to have the pristine Splunk app code in default, and any configuration changes or changes specific to the environment are then placed in the local directory. These default and local folders are also set up in the system-specific and user-specific files. This is where Splunk file precedence comes in. When Splunk wants to display a specific XML file, it will look through the following file precedence, looking through the default directory before the local directory in each, in the following order:

- System files
- App-specific files
- User-specific files

In our example that we have been using to create our NASA squid and web data app, we know that we have placed everything in this location:

`$SPLUNK_HOME/etc/apps/nasa_squid_web/local/data/ui/views/nasa_web_data.xml`

For Splunk to display this though, it will run through the following file precedence to find our XML data:

- `$SPLUNK_HOME/etc/system/default/data/ui/views/nasa_web_data.xml`
- `$SPLUNK_HOME/etc/system/local/data/ui/views/nasa_web_data.xml`
- `$SPLUNK_HOME/etc/apps/nasa_squid_web/default/data/ui/views/nasa_web_data.xml`
- `$SPLUNK_HOME/etc/apps/nasa_squid_web/local/data/ui/views/nasa_web_data.xml`
- `$SPLUNK_HOME/etc/users/username/default/data/ui/views/nasa_web_data.xml`
- `$SPLUNK_HOME/etc/users/username/local/data/ui/views/nasa_web_data.xml`

So, if you accidentally duplicate your SimpleXML file in a different location or have switched from making changes on the server to making changes through the code editor, you may be making changes to a file but Splunk may be displaying a file it has found earlier in our file precedence.

When we discuss how Splunk caches data, we need to know that Splunk app files, configuration files, and static files are cached on both the client and the server, which means any time you make changes to any of these source files, you will need to make sure that you clear both the client and server cache. Restarting Splunk will always clear the cache, but in some cases, you don't need to go that far. If you are updating views, including both Simple XML and configuration files, all you need to do is enter the URL in your browser: `http://<host:port>/debug/refresh`.

The following image is an example of what you will see when Splunk performs a refresh of your environment to allow changes to take effect:

```
Entity refresh control page
=============================
' ' '
Forces a refresh on splunkd resources

        This method calls a splunkd refresh on all registered EAI handlers that
        advertise a reload function.  Alternate entities can be specified by appending
        them via URI parameters.  For example,

            http://localhost:8000/debug/refresh?entity=admin/conf-times&entity=data/ui/manager

        will request a refresh on only 'admin/conf-times' and 'data/ui/manager'.

        1) not all splunkd endpoints support refreshing.
        2) auth-services is excluded from the default set, as refreshing that system will
           logout the current user; use the 'entity' param to force it
' ' '

Refreshing admin/conf-times            OK
Refreshing data/ui/manager             OK
Refreshing data/ui/nav                 OK
Refreshing data/ui/views               OK
Refreshing admin/alert_actions               LicenseRestriction [HTTP 402] Current license does n
Refreshing admin/clusterconfig               LicenseRestriction [HTTP 402] Current license does n
Refreshing admin/collections-conf            BadRequest
  In handler 'collections-conf': Must use user context of 'nobody' when interacting with collect
```

 You will need to refresh the cache only if you are making changes to the code directly on your server. If you are using the Splunk code editor, it will perform this change for you.

When we are setting up our development environment, we can also set up our `web.conf` file with the following configurations to make sure that the cache is disabled on splunkd:

```
cacheEntriesLimit = 0
cacheBytesLimit = 0
```

Make sure that this is changed only on your development environment and not production as this is not recommended. The Splunk cache can seem like a hinderence when developing but when providing content to your users, it does a lot of work to speed up the delivery of your visualizations to your users. Continuing to disable the cache in the production environment would cause significant degradation of services and lower the delivery of data significantly.

Getting started with the SimpleXML code

We are going to dive straight in and create another dashboard with one chart. We will create it using the Splunk web interface and then be able to view the underlying code that is created as SimpleXML:

1. Let's start by accessing our NASA squid and web data app and click on the **Dashboards** menu.
2. We want to create a new dashboard for this exercise, so we click on the **Create New Dashboard** button.
3. Set the **Title** as `SimpleXMLDashboard` and click on the **Create Dashboard** button.

In this example, we want to search for all the requests that have been made to the NASA website for movies from educational domains, using the following as our search:

```
index=main sourcetype=NASASquidLogs | search movies | search edu | top
5 From
```

From within your new `SimpleXMLDashboard`:

1. Click on **Edit** and select **Edit Panels.**
2. Click on the **Add Panel** button and select **New**, and then choose **Bar** for a bar chart.

3. Set the details of the chart to the following values:
   - **Content Title**: **Education Usage**
   - **Search String**: `index=mainsourcetype=NASASquidLogs | search movies | search edu | top 5 From`
4. Click on the **Add to Dashboard** button.
5. Then click on **Done.**

This should leave you with the following bar chart on your new dashboard:

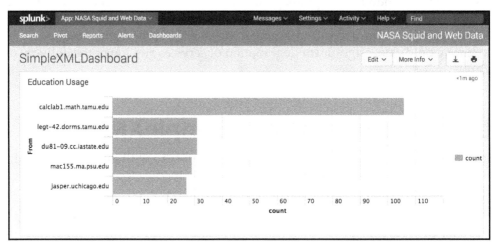

As we stated earlier, the underlying code for all the visualizations we have created in the Splunk web interface, including this new chart, is SimpleXML. To show this, we can open the chart we have created in the Splunk code editor and view the SimpleXML firsthand:

1. This time, we use the **Edit** button to edit our dashboard.
2. Select **Edit Source**.

If everything has worked the way you hoped, you should see a similar screenshot to the one displayed previously, which is the Splunk code editor screen. The first thing you are probably thinking of is that there is not a lot of code for the entire dashboard that we have just created, and I hope you are thinking that the code itself doesn't look too scary at all. So let's break down the code and try and clarify this all for you.

In the following section, you can see that the first two lines specify our root element for all our views, which is a dashboard. Make note that we can also include additional values in this `dashboard` tag, including scripts and style sheets, but we will look at that later. The next tag is a `label` tag, which gives our dashboard a name. We can also include a `description` tag and the `label` tag if we want to:

```
1 <dashboard>
2   <label>SimpleXMLDashboard</label>
```

From the third line of the code onward is where things get a little more interesting. You will see that our dashboard includes a row and our row includes a panel in line 4. Panels are containers that group one or more visualizations together. In this instance, we can see that our panel includes a chart with a title on line 6, and a query for a search on line 8 with the type of chart specified as an option in line 12:

```
3    <row>
4      <panel>
5        <chart>
6          <title>Education Usage</title>
7          <search>
8            <query>index=main sourcetype=NASASquidLogs | search
               movies | search edu | top 5 From</query>
9            <earliest>0</earliest>
10           <latest></latest>
11         </search>
12         <option name="charting.chart">bar</option>
13         <option
           name="charting.axisY2.enabled">undefined</option>
```

Throughout the code, we can see that all the tag elements have an opening element and a closing element, specified with a forward slash (/). The remaining four lines of the code are closing off the chart, panel, row, and dashboard elements of the dashboard we created:

```
14         </chart>
15       </panel>
16     </row>
17 </dashboard>
```

The Splunk code editor

In our example, we have seen how we can view the SimpleXML of a dashboard that was created from the Splunk web interface. We are using the Splunk code editor to view the SimpleXML code and save the changes to our dashboard. If we want to create a dashboard from scratch, we can also do that using the Splunk code editor. To create a new dashboard from scratch, we can perform the following:

1. From the top set of menus, along the right-hand side, click on **Settings**.
2. Click on the **User Interface** option, and you will be taken to the **User Interface management** screen.
3. We click on the **Views** option, where we can display all the views that we have in our Splunkenvironment, with a page similar to the image provided here:

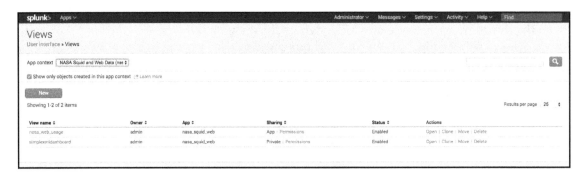

As you can see, the page gives you the ability to create a new view with the **New** button as well as manage and configure existing views that have been created. When editing or creating a new view, we will be presented with the Splunk code editor, to allow us to make the changes we need. So let's perform a quick exercise to create the most basic view that we can:

1. Within the **Views management** page, we make sure that the **App** context, near the top left of the screen is set to our NASA squid and web data app.
2. Click on the **New** button to create a new view and you will be presented with the Splunk code editor, as you were previously.

3. To create your new view, enter these details:
   - **Destination app**: `nasa_squid_web`
   - **View name**: `basic_dashboard`
   - Enter the following in the code area:

```
1 <dashboard>
2    <label>Basic Dashboard</label>
3 </dashboard>
```

4. The Splunk code editor should look the same as what is shown in the following screenshot. As you are typing the code, you will notice that although the editor is basic, it is still color coded. It highlights errors and element tags that are not closed off correctly, and indents your code to make it more readable. So when you are happy with your new view, click on the **Save** button.

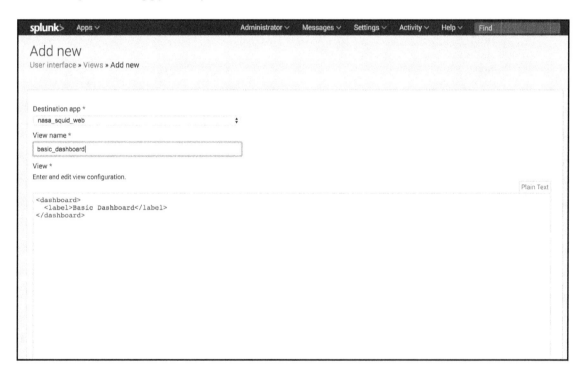

When you go back to the NASA squid and web data app, you can open your new **Basic Dashboard**. You have a boring, empty page without any real information. Just remember though that you used only three lines of code to create it.

Don't worry; the rest of this chapter is going to be dedicated to using SimpleXML to create and configure some common visualizations within Splunk.

We have made a few changes to our Splunk app that have not been committed to our Git repository. If you have created your new dashboards by sharing them within your NASA squid and web data app, you will be able to access your Splunk apps directory on your Splunk server and see that there are a few changes that you have not added to your repository yet. If you perform a status check, you will be able to see something similar to the following code:

```
nasa_squid_web$ git status

On branch master
Your branch is up-to-date with 'origin/master'.
Changes not staged for commit:
  (use "git add <file>..." to update what will be committed)
  (use "git checkout -- <file>..." to discard changes in working directory)

    modified:   metadata/local.meta

Untracked files:
  (use "git add <file>..." to include in what will be committed)

    local/data/ui/views/basic_dashboard.xml
    local/data/ui/views/simplexmldashboard.xml

no changes added to commit (use "git add" and/or "git commit -a")
```

As you can see in the output from our Splunk environment, our two new dashboards that we created are currently not tracked. To add it to our master code in Git, all we need to do is add, commit, and then push our changes back to GitHub with the following:

1. Access our Splunk server and move to our Splunk app directory:

   cd $SPLUNK_HOME/etc/apps/nasa_squid_web

2. Add all the changes you have made to allow Git to track changes; this will include the new dashboards you have created:

   git add .

3. Now commit the changes with a short description of the changes:

```
git commit -m "Adding new dashboards to splunk app"
```

4. Push your changes back to GitHub:

```
git push -u origin
```

In the next part of this chapter, we are going to expand our knowledge of SimpleXML, but we will be moving back to our discussion on the development process and start by creating a development branch for the changes we are going to make to our Splunk app.

Create development branches with Git

As we expand our knowledge of the Splunk web interface, we need to remember that we can't continue to make changes directly on our production environment. By now, we would have our development environment set up and can use the Splunk code editor or our favorite code editor to make changes and enhancements to our Splunk app without affecting our users on production. This is where branching will also help, as it means that we can create a separate development branch for each release or upgrade and each developer can create their own branch to separate their work further.

In our example, we may have one developer adding features to the Simple XML dashboard and another developer adding features to the NASA Web Usage dashboard. Both developers would be able to create their own branch, perform development, test, then merge into the master code, and then release to production.

For now, we will create a new branch of our code as we want to expand our Simple XML dashboard. The easiest way to do this is to go to your GitHub web interface and from within your repository, do these steps:

1. Access your repository page from GitHub.
2. Click on the **Branch** button, and a menu will drop down.

3. This will allow you to either search for a branch or create a new branch, as we have shown in the following screenshot. From within the text box, enter the name of your branch. In this instance, it will be called `feature-simplexml`:

4. That's all we need to do to create a branch, but unfortunately, our development environment does not know about this change yet. All we need to do is pull this change to our development environment:

```
git pull
From github.com:vincesesto/nasa_squid_web_data
* [new branch]       feature-simplexml -> origin/feature-
  simplexml
Already up-to-date.
```

5. Our development environment is now aware that there is a new branch, and we can change to this branch by using the `checkout` command along with the name of our new branch:

```
git checkout feature-simplexml
```

6. Lastly, if we ever want to know what branch we are currently working on, we can use the `branch` command, with the asterisk denoting the branch we are working on:

```
git branch
* feature-simplexml
      master
```

Adding charts to dashboards

We now have a development branch to work from and we are now going to work further with the SimpleXMLDashboard dashboard. We should already be on our development server environment as we have just switched over to our new development branch. We are going to create a new bar chart showing the daily NASA site access for our top educational user. We will change the label of the dashboard, and finally we will place an average overlay on top of our chart:

1. We go into the local directory of our Splunk App, and into the views directory where all our Simple XML code is for all our dashboards:

   cd $SPLUNK_HOME/etc/apps/nasa_squid_web/local/data/ui/views

2. We are going to work on the `simplexmldashboard.xml` file. Open this file with a text editor or your favorite code editor. Don't forget that you can also use the Splunk Code Editor if you are not comfortable with the other methods.

   It is not compulsory to indent and nest your Simple XML code, but it is a good idea to have consistent indentation and commenting to make sure your code is clear and stays as readable as possible.

3. Let's start by changing the name of the dashboard that is displayed to the user. Change line 2 to the following line of code (don't include the line numbers):

   ```
   2   <label>Educational Site Access</label>
   ```

4. Move down to line 16 and you will see that we have closed off our row element with a `</row>` element. We are going to add in a new row where we will place our new chart. After line 16, we add the following three lines to create a new row element and a new panel to add our chart. Finally, we open up our new chart element:

```
17   <row>
18     <panel>
19       <chart>
```

5. The next two lines will give our chart a title and we can then open up our search:

```
20           <title>Top Educational User</title>
21           <search>
```

6. To create a new search, just like we would enter in the Splunk search bar, we will use the `query` tag as listed with our next line of code. In our search element, we can also set the earliest and latest times for our search, but in this instance we are using the entire data source:

```
22                   <query>index=main sourcetype=nasasquidlogs
                     | search calclab1.math.tamu.edu | stats
                     count by MonthDay </query>
23           <earliest>0</earliest>
24           <latest></latest>
25         </search>
```

7. We have completed our search and we can now modify the way the chart will look on our panel with the option chart elements. In our next four lines of code, we set the chart type as column chart, set the legend to the bottom of the chart area, remove any master legend, and finally set the height as 250 pixels:

```
26           <option name="charting.chart">column</option>
27           <option
             name="charting.legend.placement">bottom</option>
28           <option
             name="charting.legend.masterLegend">null</option>
29           <option name="height">250px</option>
```

8. Finally, we need to close off the chart, panel, row and dashboard elements. Make sure you only close off the dashboard element once:

```
30          </chart>
31        </panel>
32      </row>
33 </dashboard>
```

9. We have done a lot of work here. We should be saving and testing our code for every 20 or so lines that we add, so save your changes. And as we mentioned earlier in the chapter, we want to refresh our cache by entering the following URL in our browser: `http://<host:port>/debug/refresh`.

10. When we view our page, we should see a new column chart at the bottom of our dashboard showing the usage per day for the `calclab1.math.tamu.edu` domain.

11. But we're not done with that chart yet. We want to put a line overlay showing the average site access per day for our user. Open up the `simplexmldashboard.xml` file again and change the query in line 22 to the following:

```
22    <query>index=main sourcetype=nasasquidlogs | search
      calclab1.math.tamu.edu | stats count by MonthDay|
      eventstats avg(count) as average | eval
      average=round(average,0)</query>
```

Simple XML contains some special characters, which are ', <, >, and &. If you intend to use advanced search queries, you may need to use these characters, and if so, you can do so by either using their HTML entity or using the CDATA tags, where you can wrap your query with `<![CDATA[` and `]]>`.

12. We now need to add two new option lines into our Simple XML code. After line 29, add the following new lines without replacing all the closing elements that we previously entered. The first will set the chart overlay field to be displayed for the average field, the next will set the color of the overlay:

```
30    <option
      name="charting.chart.overlayFields">average</option>
31    <option name="charting.fieldColors">{"count": 0x639BF1,
      "average":0xFF5A09}</option>
```

13. Save your new changes, refresh the cache, and then reload your page. You should be seeing somethingsimilar to the following screenshot:

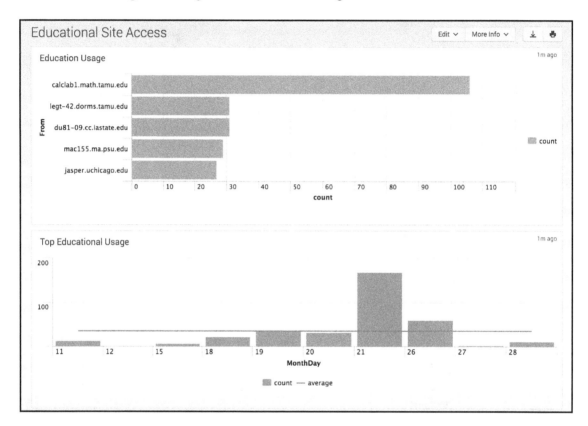

The Simple XML of charts

As we can see from our example, it is relatively easy to create and configure our charts using Simple XML. When we completed the chart, we used five options to configure the look and feel of the chart, but there are many more that we can choose from.

Our chart element always needs to be between its two parent elements, which are row and panel. Within our chart element, we always start with a title for the chart and a search to power the chart. We can then make additional optional settings for earliest and latest, and then a list of options to configure the look and feel we have demonstrated as follows. If these options are not specified, default values are provided by Splunk:

```
1    <chart>
2      <title></title>
3      <search>
4        <query></query>
5        <earliest>0</earliest>
6        <latest></latest>
7      </search>
8      <option name=""></option>
9    </chart>
```

There is a long list of options that can be set for our charts; the following is a list of the more important options to know:

- **charting.chart**: This is where you set the chart type, with area, bar, bubble, column, fillerGauge, line, markerGauge, pie, radialGauge, and scatter being the charts that you can choose from.
- **charting.backgroudColor**: Set the background color of your chart to a Hex color value.
- **charting.drilldown**: Set to either all or none. This allows the chart to be clicked on to allow the search to be drilled down for further information.
- **charting.fieldColors**: This can map a color to a field, as we did with our average field in the previous example.
- **charting.fontColor**: Set the value of the font color in the chart with a Hex color value.
- **height**: The height of the chart in pixels. The value must be between 100 and 1,000 pixels.

Many of the options seem to be self-explanatory, but a full list of options and a description can be found on the Splunk reference material at the following URL:

```
http://docs.splunk.com/Documentation/Splunk/latest/Viz/ChartConfigurationRef
erence
```

Expanding our Splunk app with maps

We will now go through another example in our NASA Squid and Web Data App to run through a more complex type of visualization to present to our user. We will use the Basic Dashboard that we created, but we will change the Simple XML to give it a more meaningful name, and then set up a map to present to our users where our requests are actually coming from. Maps use a map element and don't rely on the chart element as we have been using.

The Simple XML code for the dashboard we created earlier in this chapter looks like this:

```
<dashboard>
  <label>Basic Dashboard</label>
</dashboard>
```

So let's get to work and give our Basic Dashboard a little "bling":

1. We go into the local directory of our Splunk App, and into the views directory where all our Simple XML code is present for our Basic Dashboard:

   cd $SPLUNK_HOME/etc/apps/nasa_squid_web/local/data/ui/views

2. Open the `basic_dashboard.xml` file with a text editor or your favorite code editor. Don't forget that you can also use the Splunk Code Editor if you are not comfortable with other methods.

3. We might as well remove all of the code that is in there, because it is going to look completely different than the way it did originally.

4. Now start by setting up your dashboard and label elements with a label that will give you more information on what the dashboard contains:

   ```
   1 <dashboard>
   2   <label>Show Me Your Maps</label>
   ```

5. Now open your `row`, `panel`, and `map` elements, and set a title for the new visualization. Make sure you use the `map` element and not the chart element:

```
3    <row>
4      <panel>
5        <map>
6          <title>User Locations</title>
```

6. We can now add our search query within our search elements. We will only search for IP addresses in our data and use the geostats Splunk function to extract a latitude and longitude from the data:

```
7          <search>
8            <query>index=main sourcetype="nasasquidlogs" |
             search From=1* | iplocation From | geostats
             latfield=lat longfield=lon count by From</query>
9            <earliest>0</earliest>
10           <latest></latest>
11         </search>
```

The search query that we have in our Simple XML code is more advanced than the previous queries we have implemented. If you need further details on the functions provided in the query, please refer to the Splunk search documentation at the following location: `http://docs.splunk.com` `/Documentation/Splunk/6.4.1/SearchReference/WhatsInThisManual.`

7. Now all we need to do is close off all our elements, and that's all that is needed to create our new visualization of IP address requests:

```
12         </map>
13       </panel>
14     </row>
15 </dashboard>
```

If your dashboard looks similar to the following screenshot, I think it looks pretty good. But there is more we can do with our code to make it look even better. We can set extra options in our Simple XML code to zoom in, only display a certain part of the map, set the size of the markers, and finally set the minimum and maximum that can be zoomed into the screen.

The map looks pretty good, but it seems that a lot of the traffic is being generated by users in USA. Let's have a look at setting some extra configurations in our Simple XML to change the way the map displays to our users. We get back to our `basic_dashboard.xml` file and add the following options:

1. After our search element is closed off, we can add the following options. First, we will set the maximum clusters to be displayed on our map as 100. This will hopefully speed up our map being displayed and allow all the data points to be viewed further with the `drilldown` option:

```
12    <option
      name="mapping.data.maxClusters">100</option>
13    <option name="mapping.drilldown">all</option>
```

2. We can now set our central point for the map to load using latitude and longitude values. In this instance, we are going to set the heart of USA as our central point, we are also going to set our zoom value as 4, which will zoom in a little further than the default of 2:

```
14      <option name="mapping.map.center">(38.48,-102)
        </option>
15      <option name="mapping.map.zoom">4</option>
```

3. Remember that we need to have our map, panel, row and dashboard elements closed off. Save the changes and reload the cache, and let's see what is now displayed:

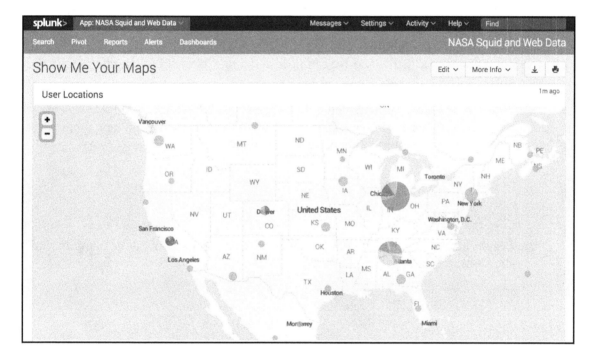

Your map should now as well as displaying a little faster than what it originally did. It will be focused on USA, where a bulk of the traffic is coming from. The map element has numerous options to use and configure and a full list can be found at the following Splunk reference page:

```
http://docs.splunk.com/Documentation/Splunk/latest/Viz/PanelreferenceforSimp
lifiedXML
```

Finally, a table!

Our dashboard is looking really good, but we just want to add one more change to our Simple XML code for the Basic Dashboard. We want to add a table at the bottom of the page showing the top five countries using the website, so that our users accessing our Splunk App will know that the site is being accessed by countries other than USA. So we open up our `basic_dashboard.xml` file, and we can now add a new element to our charts with the table element:

1. After our row for our map element has been closed off, we want to add a new row straight after that, so we start by adding our row, panel, and new table element. Let's also add a title name for the table:

```
19    <row>
20      <panel>
21        <table>
22          <title>Top 5 Countries</title>
```

2. We set up the search element and the query that we are going to be using to find the country location from our IP address:

```
23            <search>
24              <query>index=main sourcetype="nasasquidlogs" |
                search From=1* | stats count by From |
                iplocation From | top 5 Country</query>
25              <earliest>0</earliest>
26            </search>
```

3. Finally, close off your table, panel, row, and dashboard elements:

```
27        </table>
28        </panel>
29     </row>
30 </dashboard>
```

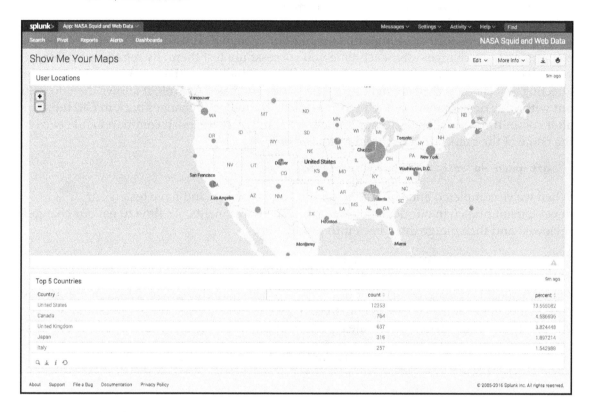

I am hoping that by now you are seeing how easy and quick it is to get your dashboards running by using Simple XML. We have set up a fully functional dashboard, providing some impressive visualizations with only 30 lines of code. And when you get more confident with using Simple XML, you will see that it is actually quicker and easier than using the Splunk Web Interface.

Completing your development and releasing to production

By now, you should have quite a few modified files in your development branch. As part of your development process, you should be committing changes and pushing them back to GitHub on a regular basis. As we discussed earlier in this chapter, you should be testing your code after every 20 or so lines that you add or change in your code. You should also be committing your changes after each time you successfully test them. By regularly pushing your changes to GitHub, it allows other developers to make sure that your work is not affecting any changes they are making to the same code base. As well, it allows them to help out with your development branch when needed. To push our changes back to GitHub, after committing our changes to our branch, we simply use the push command and specify the name of the branch that we are developing on:

```
git push -u origin feature-simplexml
```

When we've completed and committed all our code changes, and have tested our development branch in our development and test environments, it's time to get our changes reviewed and then merge them back into production.

The best way to get our code reviewed is by submitting a Pull request for our branch within GitHub. By submitting a pull request in GitHub, it gives developers the ability to send a request to colleagues or other developers to view the changes and see if there are any potential issues that may have been missed. It also lets developers suggest potential ways of enhancing our code further. To create a pull request, we can do the following:

1. We access our repository page in GitHub and click on the **New Pull Request** button.

2. We should now see a similar page to the following screenshot. The reason behind the `pull` request is to compare our branch and the master code. As you can see in the following screenshot, we can choose the base as master (or any other branch) and then select our `feature-simplexml` branch from the drop-down list to compare with:

3. By selecting our branch, we are then able to give our pull request a meaningful title. There is also a comment area to allow you to leave a list of changes you have made to your code.

4. Then click on the **Create Pull Request** button. Once the pull request is created, we can see that our pull request has been given a number. Most likely, for our first pull request, it will be #1. The following screenshot is what your pullrequest should look like:

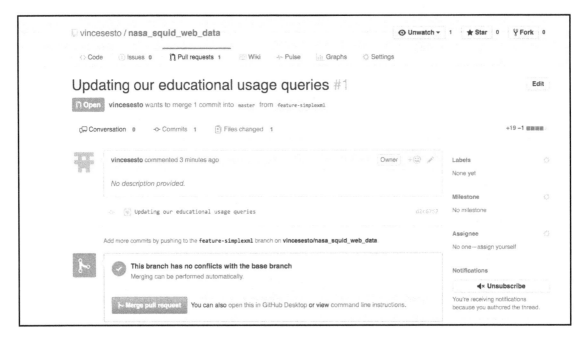

5. Any developers who are set as watchers will be notified of the pull request and you can also send the URL out to other developers for them to view.

6. By clicking on the **Files Changed** tab of the pull request, you are able to see a breakdown of all the changes made compared to the master branch. Comments can be made directly on the code pages and to the entire pull request. Changes and comments can also be voted on.

7. As you can see from our pull request, we are also given the option to **Merge pull** request. This is the final step in the process before we release our master branch into production.

8. Once we confirm that we are merging our pull request, we are given the opportunity to delete the branch, as this is usually a best practice to keep our repository clean and limit the number of branches we create.

We are now able to release our changes to our production environment. In this instance, we would simply access our production Splunk Server, locate our Splunk App directory, and then perform a Git pull.

This will now pull down all the changes we have made to our development branch that have now been merged back into our master code. All that would be left would be to restart our Splunk Server to allow the changes to take effect.

Summary

In this chapter, we continued to work with our new Splunk App but we moved on to developing our interface with Simple XML. We learned what Simple XML was and how to view the underlying Simple XML code for our application dashboards and views via the Splunk Code Editor. We continued to work on our example application, where we added more features to our interface using the Simple XML code and provided a breakdown of the different parts of the code and the options we can use to further configure the look and feel of the interface.

We continued to work with our Splunk Server and discussed the way Splunk uses precedence to display our Splunk App visualizations. We also looked at the way Splunk uses caching and what we need to do to work around this feature while developing our code. We learned how to create branches in our Git repository to further expand our development process and provide a way for development to continue on without causing changes and potential bugs on our master code.

Coming up, we are going to continue to work with Simple XML and learn how to create and manipulate menus within Splunk Apps, as well as configure the layout of our panels and charts presented to our users. We will add new dashboards to our NASA Squid and Web Data Splunk App as well as introduce a new example where we look at a biological cell simulation and how we can present this information to our users.

4

Layouts, Navigation, and Menus

We are starting to really make some progress with our knowledge and it is starting to show as our SplunkApp is looking better with each development iteration. There is one thing we need to be mindful of; as well as delivering information that the end user is going to find useful, we also need to put it in a format whereby the user will be able to view the data readily and have it presented to them in a format that is easy on the eye, draws them in, and gets them to want more.

This is where our layouts, navigation, and menus come into play. Most of our users these days will have used a computer and had exposure to a menu select interface, but you may have quite a few users who have not used Splunk before. So, having them search around for dashboards becomes a deterrent to having them use the reports that you have spent so much time creating. We also need to draw our users into reports, and this is where the layout of the dashboard panels can either confuse them or have them wanting more.

In this chapter we will focus on layouts, navigation, and menus, as well as practising the skills that we have learnt already in the previous chapters by setting up our new example Splunk App. In this chapter, we will learn these topics:

- How to work with the Splunk App's navigation XML file
- Setting the default dashboard of our Splunk App as well as manipulating the menu structure presented to our users
- How to change the way our dashboard panels are set out and how to combine panels to allow our data to be grouped together more logically
- We will also introduce JavaScript and CSS static files to our Splunk App to add extra flexability to our layouts
- We will change the colors of our text and visualizations based on search results

By setting up navigation and menus, we take our Splunk App from a prototype to a professional and fully functional release ready for production users. So, we will look at the menu of our NASA Squid and Web Data App to give it that finishing touch before we start with our second example.

Setting your Splunk app's default page

I have mentioned previously that Splunk does not offer a way for you to set the default page or dashboard to be displayed for your Splunk App through the Web Interface. You should be a lot more familiar with the Simple XML code in Splunk, and by manipulating the navigation directory of our Simple XML, we will be able to provide our dashboard as the first thing that our users will see.

There are two ways to manipulate the Simple XML that will control our navigation and menu for our Splunk App, either through the Splunk Code Editor or by making the changes directly on the server through our own text or code editor. Either way, the changes that are being made to the Simple XML will be the same. So, the first change we will make will be through the Splunk Code Editor:

1. We've been using Git for a while now and as we have started a new piece of work on our SplunkApp, we create a new branch and start working with our development environment.
2. Log in to your development environment and access the **Settings** menu at the top right of the screen. Then select **User interface**.
3. Select **Navigation Menus** from the list of operations you can perform and you will be presented with the following screen:

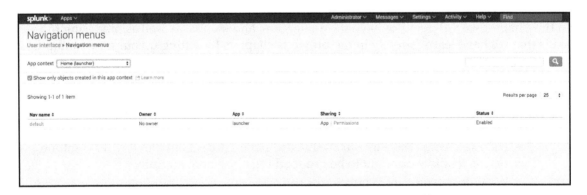

4. From the **App context** drop-down list, select the **Splunk App** that the navigation menu will refer to. In this case, we will continue to work on our example, the NASA Squid and Web Data App.

5. You will only have one navigation provided in the list, and it will be called default. Click on this **Nav** to open it. You will be presented with the following code:

```
1 <nav search_view="search" color="#65A637">
2   <view name="search" default='true' />
3   <view name="pivot" />
4   <view name="reports" />
5   <view name="alerts" />
6   <view name="dashboards" />
7 </nav>
```

6. As you can see, the code is enclosed in `nav` elements, with each dashboard added using the view element. We can also see that the color and the default page to be displayed are being controlled by this code.

7. To add our new NASA Web Usage dashboard to the list of views at the top of the screen and to set it as the default page, first we need to stop the main search page from being the default page. Edit the second line of the Simple XML to look like the following code:

```
2   <view name="search" />
```

8. We have removed the search page from being displayed as the default dashboard, we now need to add the NASA Web Usage dashboard as default, so we will edit the last line of the code to look like this:

```
7   <view name="nasa_web_usage" default='true' />
8 </nav>
```

9. Remember to close off the `nav` element as you can see in the last line of the preceding code and click on the **Save** button. If we go to directly open our NASA Squid and Web Data Splunk App, it now opens directly in our NASA Web Usage dashboard, and we also have a new menu option with the name of our dashboard.

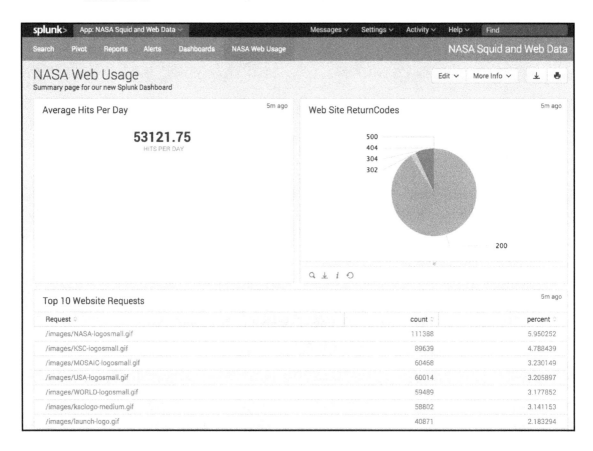

Manipulating the menu structure

We have put in place a way to access one of our new dashboards without having to do this in the **Dashboards** menu, but we can take this further and place the rest of our dashboards as menu items across the top of our screen. We can also move the original menu items of search, pivot, alerts, reports and dashboards under one drop down menu. There is not a lot of work to get this done, but we will start over, in this exercise we will make the changes on our development server environment through a text editor or your favorite code editor:

1. Log into your development environment and as we have already made some changes to our navigation, the most up to date version of our navigation will be moved to our local directory from the default. To access our navigation, change into the following directory:

   cd $SPLUNK_HOME/etc/apps/nasa_squid_web/local/data/ui/nav/

 As we have discussed previously, if you have not made changes to your navigation files, you would change to the default directory of your Splunk App at the following location: cd
$SPLUNK_HOME/etc/apps/nasa_squid_web/default/data/ui/nav/.

2. Open the default.xml file with a text editor or your favorite code editor and we can get started with our changes.

3. Remove all the lines, and we are going to start from scratch with the following four lines to open our nav element. The first line will remain the same, and as our search view will remain as search, but we will move our three main dashboards that we created following from that.

```
1  <nav search_view="search" color="#65A637">
2    <view name="nasa_web_usage" default='true' />
3    <view name="simplexmldashboard" />
4    <view name="basic_dashboard" />
```

4. Our nasa_web_usage dashboard will remain as the default dashboard to be displayed when the SplunkApp is loaded and keeps the default=true option.

5. We now want to set up the old menu items and group them together in a drop-down menu. This is where we can use the collection element. Enter the following line of code, where we open the collection element and give it the label option of `Splunk Tools`:

```
5    <collection label="Splunk Tools" >
```

6. We can then add the rest of the menu items that will be displayed in the drop down menu with the next five lines:

```
6        <view name="search" />
7        <view name="pivot" />
8        <view name="reports" />
9        <view name="alerts" />
10       <view name="dashboards" />
```

7. We are not finished yet. We want to add in a link to the current NASA website, but we want to separate it from the the other items in our drop-down menu. This is where we can use the `divider` element. Then create a link to the `http://www.nasa.gov/` website site with a `href` tag, as we would with HTML script.

```
11       <divider />
12       <a href="https://www.nasa.gov/">NASA Website</a>
```

8. Finally, all we need to do is close off the collection and `nav` elements:

```
13    </collection>
14 </nav>
```

9. Save our changes and then clear the Splunk cache, as we have in previous chapters, by entering the following url into our browser: `http://<host:port>/debug/refresh`

If we have a long list of dashboards that we created to our Splunk App, instead of having to list them all one by one we could use the following element in our navigation file and it would list them all out for us: `<saved source="unclassified" />`.

We have done a lot of work here, and if all works to plan we should be seeing a page similar to the following screenshot. We have our dashboard labels used as the menu items across the top of the SplunkApp. The last menu item also has a downwards arrow, which gives us an indication that there is a drop-down menu, and in this instance the remaining Splunk tools that we added and the current NASA website link divided from the other menu options.

If you need further information on the navigation menu within Splunk Simple XML, it can be found in the reference documentation at the link: `http://docs.splunk.com/Documentation/Splunk/latest/AdvancedDev/BuildNavigation`.

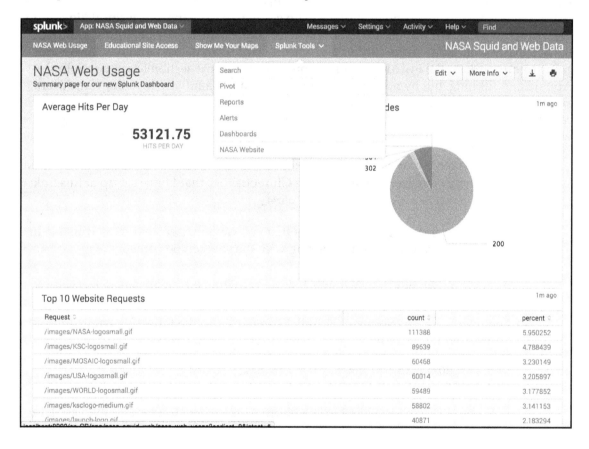

Commit your changes, and push them back to GitHub. Deploy to your test environment, test, and deploy to your production environment. We have taken our NASA Squid and Web Data App as far as we will in this book, and it's time for us to move onto our second example, where we use Splunk to create an App to view a biological simulation of cell growth.

Biological cell simulation app

It's now time to start on our second example Splunk App. As we discussed in the first chapter of this book, the second example we are going to be looking at is a simulation of cell growth across time. We will use this example to continue learning about Simple XML; then we will expand our knowledge further and start to work with dashboard layouts. We are going to run through the instructions pretty quickly in the next section to get our Splunk App up and running, but by now you should be a lot more familiar with using Git, Splunk, and Simple XML. For our new Splunk App, we want to create a dashboard that provides cell counts to our users in the form of single-value elements, so let's start to set that up. As we go, we will learn some of the important aspects of Simple XML layout elements:

1. If you haven't done so already, access the `game_of_life.log` file from the Packt Publishing code website or from the Git repository that I have set up at this link: `https://github.com/vincesesto/game_of_life_splunk`.

2. Set up your indexing and make sure that you can now see your data available in Splunk. We have set up our indexing with the sourcetype named `cellsimulation`.

3. As we did with our first example, log in to GitHub and create a new repository called `cell_biology`.

4. Log on to your development Splunk Server and run the following command to create your new Splunk App:

```
$SPLUNK_HOME/bin/splunk create app cell_biology -template
barebones
```

5. We should now have a barebones Splunk App created, but let's double-check by changing into our new Splunk App:

```
cd $SPLUNK_HOME/etc/apps/cell_biology/
```

6. We should have our new Splunk App structure set up and ready to be committed to our Git repository. Run the following Git commands from the `cell_biology` directory. To initialize, add your new directories and files and then commit the changes:

```
git init
git add .
git commit -m "Setting up our new cell simulation app"
```

7. We can now set up the remote location of our Git repository back to GitHub. Make sure to substitute <account> in the following command with your account name:

```
git remote add origin git@github.com:
<account>/cell_biology.git
```

8. And now push the changes back to GitHub:

```
git push -u origin master
```

9. You should be able to access your GitHub account and your new repository will be filled with your new Splunk App. If you log on to your development Splunk environment, you will also be able to see that you now have a new Splunk App called `cell_biology`.

Let's keep going and make sure our new Splunk App displays a nicer name in the Splunk interface, as well as getting a new dashboard up and running:

1. We have set up the new Splunk App, but it is displaying the name on the Web Interface of `cell_biology`. We can correct this by amending the `app.conf` file. As we are going to be working directly with the development server, this file will be located in the default directory and not in the local directory. So, change to the default directory of your development environment:

```
cd $SPLUNK_HOME/etc/apps/cell_biology/default
```

2. Open the `app.conf` file, locate the `[ui]` section of the file, and change the label of `cell_biology` to something similar to the following:

```
8 [ui]
9 is_visible = true
10 label = Cell Biology
```

3. Notice that in this file we can also set version numbers for our Splunk App and other information surrounding our app, author, and licenses. We will use this file a little more in the next chapter when we have a look at packaging up our Splunk App.

4. We can now set up a new dashboard, which will give us a break down of the number of times certain cell groups appear. First we change to our views directory so that we can create our new dashboard:

```
cd $SPLUNK_HOME/etc/apps/cell_biology/default/data/ui/views/
```

5. Create a new file named cell_counts.xml and set up the Simple XML code as follows to open the dashboard element. Set a label and description of the dashboard and open the new row element:

```
1  <dashboard>
2    <label>Cell Simulation Counts</label>
3    <description>Show a breakdown of cells in our
     logs</description>
4    <row>
5      <panel>
```

6. The following Simple XML will create a single-value element. We will also use a search to query the raw data from our simulation for live cells, which are displayed as @. The first search we will do will be to highlight no live cells:

```
6        <single>
7          <title>Zero Cell Count</title>
8          <search>
9            <query><![CDATA[ index=main
             sourcetype=cellsimulation | eval data=_raw | rex
             field=data max_match=0 "(?<cells>\@)" | stats
             count(cells) AS Count by _time | where Count=0 |
             stats count ]]></query>
10           <earliest>0</earliest>
11           <latest></latest>
12         </search>
```

7. As we stated in our previous chapter, there are some special characters that cannot be used in Simple XML and our query, which includes the characters `<cells>`, would cause the dashboard to error if we do not enclose this query in `<![CDATA[]]>`.

8. Finally, set options for `label` and `linkview` and close off the row:

```
13              <option name="drilldown">none</option>
14              <option name="linkView">search</option>
15              <option name="underLabel">No Alive Cells</option>
16          </single>
17        </panel>
18      </row>
```

9. Let's quickly set up another single-value element in our dashboard, and this time we will try to count any instances that we see of less than 10 cells present in our simulation:

```
19      <row>
20        <panel>
21          <single>
22            <title>Small Cell Count</title>
23            <search>
24              <query><![CDATA[ index=main
                 sourcetype=cellsimulation | eval data=_raw | rex
                 field=data max_match=0 "(?<cells>\@)" | stats
                 count(cells) AS Count by _time | where Count<=10
                 | stats count ]     ]> </query>
25              <earliest>0</earliest>
26              <latest></latest>
27            </search>
28            <option name="drilldown">none</option>
29            <option name="linkView">search</option>
30            <option name="underLabel">Alive Cells</option>
31          </single>
32        </panel>
33      </row>
```

10. Don't forget to close off your dashboard with the final line of code in it:

```
34 </dashboard>
```

11. Finally, let's set up our navigation from the start and change to the `nav` directory as we did earlier in this chapter:

cd $SPLUNK_HOME/etc/apps/cell_biology/default/data/ui/nav/

12. Open the `default.xml` file in a text or code editor. We will set up our new dashboard as the default dashboard to be viewed, and we will also remove all the other menu headings except for search:

```
1 <nav search_view="search" color="#65A637">
2   <view name="cell_counts" default='true' />
3   <view name="search" />
4 </nav>
```

13. Save your changes and clear the Splunk cache. If all has gone smoothly, you should be presented with the following screenshot:

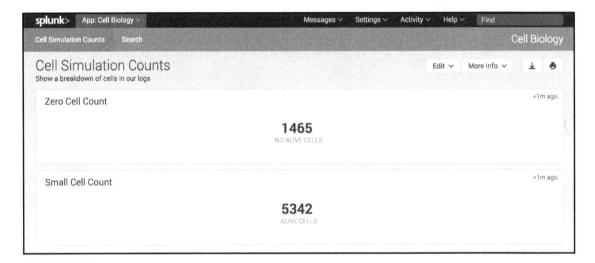

We have worked so hard to come this far, and I'm out of breath. I hope you are excited with the work that we have done, and I hope you can see how great Splunk can be to rapidly prototype your dashboards and reports. In a short period of time we have:

1. Created our new Cell Biology App.
2. Set up a new dashboard.
3. Created two visualizations for our dashboard.
4. Changed the menu system so that our new dashboard displays as our default.

Manipulating your dashboard layout

Our new dashboard is looking good, but there is a lot of wasted space that we can use a lot better. By now, you will have noticed the row elements that we have been using, and as you can well assume, each time we open the row element it also creates a new row for us. In our example, we can bunch our two single-value elements together in one row by removing the closing and opening elements in line 18 and 19 of our code. Or, instead of removing the code, we can use the comment feature of XML to comment out the two lines that we are talking about:

1. We should by now know where our dashboard is on our development environment, so open the `cell_counts.xml` file.

2. Change lines 18 and 19 to the following lines of code:

   ```
   18 <!--    </row> -->
   19 <!--    <row> -->
   ```

3. Save your changes and refresh the cache. You will now see that the two single-value elements are now displaying on a single row.

4. If we wanted to, we could continue to add single-value elements to the row, as Splunk no longer limits the number of columns that we have to three. In our example, we will also add a new single-value element, but let's see what happens when we put in some new comments in line 17 and 20 as well, so that we can combine our single-value elements into one panel.

5. Once again, open the `cell_counts.xml` file and make the following change to the code:

   ```
   17 <!--    </panel> -->
   18 <!--    </row> -->
   19 <!--    <row> -->
   20 <!--    <panel> -->
   ```

In our example, we are adding in the comment tags in each line, but if we wanted to, we could start our comment tag on one line and then end it three lines later; all the lines would then be commented out.

6. Move to the bottom of the file and remove the last two lines. Then replace it with the following lines of Simple XML to display any cell counts that are over 20 cells:

```
33      <panel>
34        <single>
35          <title>Larger Cell Count</title>
36          <search>
37            <query><![CDATA[ index=main
                sourcetype=cellsimulation | eval data=_raw | rex
                field=data max_match=0 "(?<cells>\@)" | stats
                count(cells) AS Count by _time | where Count>=20
                | stats count ]    ]> </query>
38            <earliest>0</earliest>
39            <latest></latest>
40          </search>
41          <option name="drilldown">none</option>
42          <option name="linkView">search</option>
43          <option name="underLabel">Alive Cells</option>
44        </single>
45      </panel>
46    </row>
47 </dashboard>
```

7. Save your changes, and once again refresh your cache. If all goes as planned, your dashboard should look like what is shown in the following screenshot.

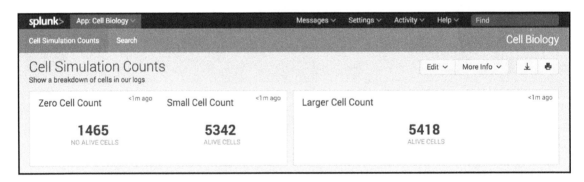

8. As we can see, the **Zero Cell Count** and **Small Cell Count** single-value elements are now displaying as a single panel that takes up the same amount of space as the **Larger Cell Count** single-value element. If we wanted to, we could remove all the panel elements in between the row elements and we would have one combined row with all three entries in place.

Customizing layouts with JavaScript

If we wanted to, we could continue to add single-value elements to the top row, but the last thing we want to do is overwhelm and confuse our users, or worse, bore them. We instead want to draw them into the dashboard to have them take more interest in the data that we are presenting to them. Instead of creating a dashboard that is perfectly symmetrical, we may want to customize the layout of the dashboard further. This is where we can start to utilize JavaScript to further enhance our layout. As we will see in later chapters, we normally use JavaScript when we start to work with HTML dashboards, but in this instance we can still use JavaScript in Simple XML code.

In the following example, we will add some extra code into our Splunk App in the form of JavaScript code to manipulate the layout, but don't worry! We will be keeping the code simple, so let's get started:

1. Access your development environment and change to the base of the Cell Biology Splunk App:

    ```
    cd $SPLUNK_HOME/etc/apps/cell_biology/
    ```

2. As we discussed in earlier chapters, Splunk has the ability to use CSS and JavaScript files located in the static directory in the `appserver` directory. We created our new Splunk App from the barebones template, so we will need to create this directory:

    ```
    mkdir appserver/static
    ```

3. Change to the static directory you have just created, create the JavaScript file called `cell_layout.js`, and start by adding the first line of code:

    ```
    1 require(['jquery', 'splunkjs/mvc/simplexml/ready!'],
        function($) {
    ```

4. This tells our code to load the jQuery and SplunkJS libraries to use as part of our code.

5. The next two lines of code will create variables of the first row and then the panels within the row:

    ```
    2     var firstRow = $('.dashboard-row').first();
    3     var panelCells = $(firstRow).children('.dashboard-
          cell');
    ```

6. Now we will set the `panelCells` variable to be be equal to 70% of the screen for the first panel and 30% for the second panel, as listed here:

```
4       $(panelCells[0]).css('width', '70%');
5       $(panelCells[1]).css('width', '30%');
```

7. We save the file, but our Simple XML does not yet know that we have made this change, and we need to open our Simple XML code again to add this new static file to our code.

8. We open the `cell_counts.xml` file that we have been working on and change the first line to the following code:

```
1 <dashboard script="cell_layout.js">
```

9. Unfortunately, changes such as this cannot be activated by simply refreshing the cache as we have been doing in the previous examples. For a change such as this to take effect, we need to restart Splunk. So restart your development environment and you should be presented with a dashboard looking similar to the following screenshot:

I know this is not a dramatic change to our interface design, but if you are anything like me, you will see yourself naturally being drawn from the left of the dashboard to the right and focusing on the **Larger Cell Count** single-value element.

Color-coding values in our display

Remember from earlier in this chapter when I was mentioning that we need to draw our user into our data? Another way we can do this is by changing the color of our data when it is at a specific value range, for example, if the data is too high or too low.

Color can be used to provide direction and draw attention to interface elements or text, but color alone should not be used to convey content. When developing an application, color should be the last thing that you implement, as you need to remember that users who cannot access color may encounter difficulties when using or viewing your application.

We can make a minor addition to the Simple XML to give our count values a different color when we receive different values. In our Cell Biology Splunk App, we can use this feature to highlight if our very first single value element, which displays no alive cells, is too high:

1. Log back into your development environment and open the `cell_counts.xml` file, which contains your main Cell Biology dashboard.

2. Change the search query on line 9 to match the following code. You will notice that we have added a new `eval` statement at the end of our search. The `eval` statement checks our count value—and if it is greater than 1,000, it will be flagged as severe—and assigns this value back to the variable class:

```
9   <query><![CDATA[ index=main sourcetype=cellsimulation |
    eval data=_raw | rex field=data max_match=0 "(?<cells>\@)"
    | stats count(cells) AS Count by _time | where Count=0 |
    stats Count | eval class=if(Count>1000,"severe","low") ]]>
    </query>
```

3. The value of `severe` is a predefined value that Splunk has set up within Simple XML to display as red; the value of `low` will display green.

4. We need to tell our display to use this value of `severe` or `low` within the options of our visualization. We can do this by using the `classField` option and setting the value the same as the `eval` statement of class. We need to add a new option to our single-value element; instead of three lines it will display the following:

```
13    <option name="classField">class</option> <!-newline -->
14    <option name="drilldown">none</option>
15    <option name="linkView">search</option>
16    <option name="underLabel">No Alive Cells</option>
```

5. We have used the value of `class` in the `classField` option, but this could be named anything as long as it matches the value in our `eval` statement in search.

6. Save your changes and refresh your Splunk cache. You should now see the **NO ALIVE CELLS** value displaying as red, potentially meaning that there may be something wrong with our simulation.

7. We have used the default values that Splunk sets for value ranges in Simple XML, where low is green, medium is black, elevated is equal to yellow, high is amber, and severe translates to red. We can also set values for our colors and color ranges using the `charting.fieldColors` option and set the values with a HEX color code. So let's add a new bar chart to our dashboard, and we will set color that is displayed for each of the bars.

8. We are going to add to our `cell_counts.xml` file again. So open up the file with your text editor in your development environment.

9. Move to the bottom of the file and delete the last line that closes off the dashboard element. We are going to create a new row with a new chart element:

```
48    <row>
49      <panel>
50        <chart>
```

10. Give our chart a title and open up the search element:

```
51    <title>Cell Count Ranges</title>
52      <search>
```

11. Our query is going to be similar to the previous cell count queries, where we are counting the number of times we see the @ symbol in a _raw data, but we are also going to set a description within three possible ranges:

```
53   <query><![CDATA[ index=main sourcetype=cellsimulation
     | eval data=_raw | rex field=data max_match=0 "(?
     <cells>\@)"
     | stats count(cells) AS Count by _time   | eval
     description=case(Count<=10, "LOW", Count<=20, "MEDIUM",
     Count>20 , "HIGH")
     | stats count(eval(description="LOW")) as LOW
     count(eval(description="MEDIUM")) as MEDIUM
     count(eval(description="HIGH")) as HIGH by description
     ]]> </query>
```

12. The preceding code would be placed in one line on your Simple XML, but I have spaced it out so it can be a little easier to read. Notice how we have set up a case statement to set the description as LOW, MEDIUM, or HIGH depending on the number of cells found in the data.

13. Close off your search:

```
54   </search>
```

14. We are now going to set the options for the chart, first setting it up as a bar chart and then using the charting.fieldColors option to set the color for LOW, MEDIUM, and HIGH:

```
55   <option name="charting.chart">bar</option>
56   <option name="charting.fieldColors">
57   {"LOW": 0xFF0000, "MEDIUM": 0xFF9900, "HIGH":0x009900,
     "NULL":0xC4C4C0}
58           </option>
```

15. We can now close off our chart, panel, row, and dashboard board elements:

```
59           </chart>
60        </panel>
61     </row>
62   </dashboard>
```

16. Save the file, refresh the cache, and load your page in your Splunk development environment.

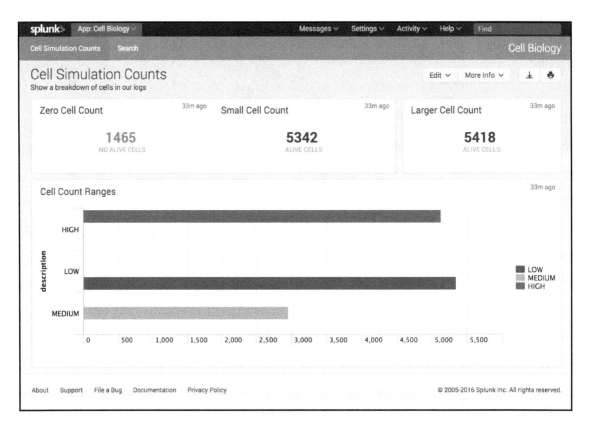

Great work! Our new chart is displaying data as we want, with different distinct colors for the LOW, MEDIUM and HIGH values in our chart. Splunk will assign its own color values to charts, and in some circumstances, this will change depending on the value returned, meaning that today our LOW value will be one color but next week it may be different. By configuring our own color values for the chart, we ensure consistency every time the report is generated. If you are looking for more information on setting up custom colors in your charts, there is a specific reference page in the Splunk documentation at the following URL:

```
http://docs.splunk.com/Documentation/Splunk/6.4./Viz/Buildandeditdashboardsw
ithSimplifiedXML#Specify_custom_colors_for_fields_in_charts.
```

Adding CSS into Simple XML

By now, we have seen that we can make minor changes to the Simple XML to create eye-catching visualizations of our data. We have also added JavaScript to our Splunk App to help us with our dashboard layouts. In the next section, we will also start to add CSS to help our JavaScript further manipulate the layout of our interface.

It may seem a little counter-productive, but we are going to duplicate the Cell Count Ranges chart that we just created. The reason behind this is that we want to show how we can provide the same data, and not just in a different format. We will combine a table and a chart using JavaScript and CSS. Although we are going to add some JavaScript and CSS, we are going to keep things pretty simple, so don't be too worried. In the following code, we are going to do this:

1. Make a change to our JavaScript file to allow it to be used in the table elements.
2. Add CSS to configure the way these changes will look.
3. We will then change our dashboard to display the new table and bar chart combination.
4. If you remember correctly, we already had a JavaScript file that we are using in our current dashboard. We are going to add another function to this code. Also, if you remember, this file is in the static directory, so let's add some more code to it.
5. We move into our static directory within our Splunk App:

   cd $SPLUNK_HOME/etc/apps/cell_biology/appserver/static

6. Open our `cell_layout.js` file with a text editor and move to the bottom of the file, as we are going to add another function to our code. We need a few more libraries in this function, so we are going to load them across multiple lines:

```
8 require([
9      'jquery',
10      'underscore',
11      'splunkjs/mvc',
12      'views/shared/results_table/renderers/
        BaseCellRenderer',
13      'splunkjs/mvc/simplexml/ready!'
```

7. The main line that we need to be concerned with here is the `BaseCellRenderer` library, as this will be the library we will use to change the way our table displays.

8. We now need to close off the `require` statement, and in this case we will also add the options of the libraries that we are going to extend:

```
14 ], function($, _, mvc, BaseCellRenderer) {
```

9. We now create a variable that extends the `BaseCellRenderer` library, specifically looking for the `percent` field, which is going to be set up in our Simple XML table:

```
15 var DataBarCellRenderer = BaseCellRenderer.extend({
16 canRender: function(cell) {
17    return (cell.field === 'percent');
18 },
```

10. The next few lines basically use our library and CSS file to make changes to the percent column to add a bar graph(`data-bar-cell`) to the table cell:

```
19 render: function($td, cell) {
20 $td.addClass('data-bar-cell').html(_.template('<div
   class="data-bar-wrapper"><div class="data-bar"
   style="width:<%- percent %>%"></div></div>', {
21    percent: Math.min(Math.max(parseFloat(cell.value), 0),
      100)
22             }));
23         }
24     });
```

11. The `mvc` library is then used to run through the components of our dashboard, specifically the table with the `id` of `tableWithBar1`, which we will add to our Simple XML shortly:

```
25 mvc.Components.get('tableWithBar1')
   \.getVisualization(function(tableView) {
26 tableView.addCellRenderer(new DataBarCellRenderer());
27     });
28 });
```

12. Save the file and create a new file that will hold our CSS information in the same directory, called `cell_layout.css`. Add the following code, which will provide us with padding for the cell, height, width and background color of the bar chart in our table:

```
1 td.data-bar-cell {
2     padding: 4px 8px;
3 }
4 td.data-bar-cell .data-bar-wrapper .data-bar {
5     height: 16px;
6     min-width: 1px;
7     background-color: #5479AF;
8 }
```

13. We save the changes, and now open our existing dashboard file in the views directory called `cell_counts.xml`. Start by changing the first line to include the new JavaScript and CSS files that we are using:

```
1   <dashboard script="cell_layout.js"
    stylesheet="cell_layout.css" >
```

14. Now move to the bottom of the file and delete the last line that closed off the dashboard element. Add in a new row element, panel and table element; and we are also going to give our table element the `id` that we created in our JavaScript file called `tableWithBar1`:

```
62    <row>
63      <panel>
64        <table id="tableWithBar1">
```

15. We add in a title for our table and open the search element ready for our new query:

```
65  <title>More Cell Count Ranges</title>
66  <search>
```

16. Our query is going to be a little different from the previous chart. It will be a little shorter and will use the top function, as we can see here:

```
67   <query><![CDATA[index=main sourcetype=cellsimulation
     | eval data=_raw
     | rex field=data max_match=0 "(?<cells>\@)"
     | stats count(cells) AS Count by _time
     | eval description=case(Count<=10    , "LOW", Count<=20,
     "MEDIUM", Count>20 , "HIGH") | top description
     ]]> </query>
```

17. Now complete the new table by closing off `search`, `table`, `panel`, and `row`, and finally close off the entire dashboard with the ending dashboard element that we removed earlier:

```
68               </search>
69             </table>
70           </panel>
71         </row>
72     </dashboard>
```

18. Save all your changes, and as we needed to do previously, we will need to restart Splunk, as this is how we can get our JavaScript and CSS changes to take effect.

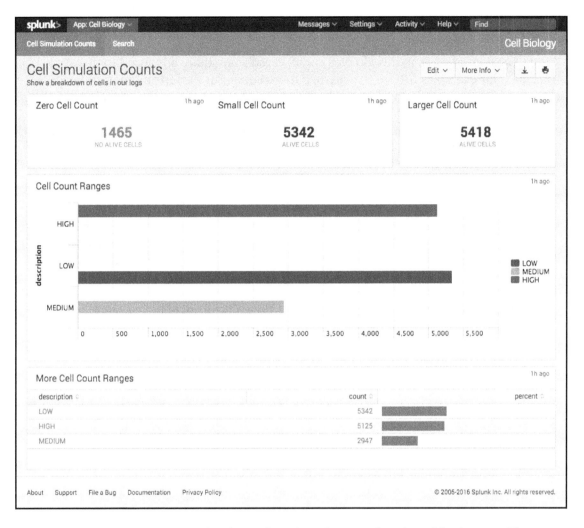

19. Our dashboard now displays a bar chart from within the table element. There are lots of examples in the Splunk reference material, so don't be worried if you are new to JavaScript and CSS. Make sure you continue to add and commit your changes to GitHub, and it's time to move on to our next chapter.

Summary

We've done a lot of work in this chapter and covered some more advanced topics. As we developed our examples further, we learned more about our design and manipulated the layouts of our dashboards. We learned how to work with the navigation Simple XML file for our Splunk App to set up a default page for our users, and configured the way our menu structure is set up and displayed to our users. We also started working with our new Biological Cell Simulation Splunk App and discovered how to change the way our visualizations are set out on our dashboards, both using Simple XML and by adding simple JavaScript and CSS to our code. We also saw how to change the color of our text and charts from the default provided by Splunk.

In our next chapter, we will continue to work with Simple XML Dashboards, and we are going to learn how to interact further with the user by implementing form-based elements. We will give users more freedom in interacting with our data by adding drilldown elements to allow them to click on chart, table, and single-value elements so that they can expand the underlying events. We will also introduce the different search elements available and set up post processing searches to speed up our visualizations on our dashboards. We will take a quick look at packaging up our Splunk App so that it can be deployed directly on other environments, or even added to the SplunkBase App repository.

5
Interacting with Your User While Speeding up App Searches

When creating an interface for our users, it is not only the look and appearance of the dashboard that is important, it is also the speed at which we present the data. It has been common knowledge since the birth of the Internet that the speed of delivery of our data will affect the experience that our users have.

This is even more important when it comes to delivering data and reports in Splunk. The amount of data that you can hold is massive, and this can always present a challenge to delivering this data in a timely manner to our users. Splunk does amazing things in the background to index, search, and deliver this data to our interface, but unfortunately, this can be lost to some users who are only concerned with the data they want to see.

This is where we are going to move on with our Splunk App development to make some minor changes to our dashboard Simple XML to speed up the delivery of the data that we present as quickly as possible.

We are also going to take steps towards giving our users the ability to start interacting with the data and allowing them to control what data is presented to the interface. In this chapter, we are going to cover these topics:

- Enhancing our user experience by introducing post-processing searchers to our dashboards to speed up searching of data
- Setting up scheduled reports and using the data from those reports to populate our dashboard panels

- Introducing Simple XML forms to our Splunk Apps to allow our users to interact directly with the data presented to them
- Customizing drilldown options within our visualizations to direct our users' searches for further information
- We finish up our Splunk App by packaging it up in the standard format, ready for distribution

Our work is going to continue with our Biological Cell Simulation Splunk App, so let's not waste any more time and get stuck straight into it.

Speeding up data delivery with post processing searches

Our main dashboard for our Cell Biology Splunk App is looking pretty good, but when we load the page, we see that there is a delay between the page displaying and our graphs and visualisations completing.

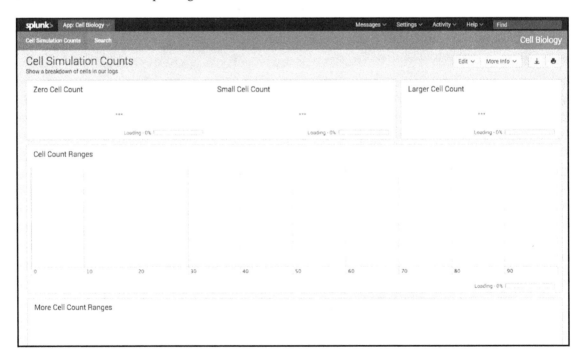

The time it takes for our search queries to complete is not that big, but in this example, we are only working with around 700 MB of data that need to be searched against. What if our cell simulations were a lot more complex? What if we were searching over larger periods of time? And what if we have terabytes of data that we need to search through to provide our report to our users? Unfortunately, some of our users, especially nontechnical users, will not really care about the technology and work going on in the background to get this data delivered. But fortunately, Splunk provides different ways for us as developers to speed up the way we deliver our data to our dashboard.

So far, our dashboard examples have been using inline searches across the visualizations, meaning that we have one main search for each panel that we are displaying. As you can see in our Cell Biology SplunkApp, all of our searches are very similar, meaning that we are duplicating a lot of work across each of the panels. The more we do this and the more panels we have with inline searches, the more the performance of our visualizations will be impacted and will slow down.

This is where postprocessing searches can help us improve the performance and speed up the display of data on our dashboard, by creating one main or *base* search for the dashboard. This base search cleans out and transforms our data to minimize the information that is then passed onto our panels, which will use postprocessing searches to then display the data we want.

Post processing searches are an effective way of conserving resources when you are using a single indexer, but they may not be as effective if you are on an environment that is using multiple indexers. It may be more effective to use multiple searches in the dashboard or, as we will see later in this chapter, refer to a scheduled search.

There are one or two limitations of using post processing in Splunk. The first is that the base search will only return the first 500,000 results, meaning that we may have incomplete data presented to our users. To work around this issue, we need to make sure that our base search is a transformational search, meaning that our base search will strip out a large amount of unwanted data before we move on to present this data further to our user. Secondly, the post processing search cannot run for longer than 30 seconds and the search will time out and cause an error on your dashboard.

In our example, we are going to use a base search for all the panels in our dashboard; then each of the panels will use a post processing search to complete their visualizations. As you can see in the layout we have presented, we use a base search that opens the specified index and source type, creates the field using a regular expression, and then transforms that data with the `stats` function. Each of the post processing searches uses that base search and feeds it through an `eval` function to look for the specific information needed for each of the visualizations required.

So for our example, we will do the following:

- Create a base search with the ID of `baseSearch`. This will search through our main index and the cell simulation sourcetype, extract our cells, and then use the `stats` function to count by time.
- Convert the searches that we previously have in our example, where they will now use the output of `baseSearch` and perform further manipulation of the data provided.

We have talked a lot, so let's get back to our development environment and start implementing the base search and post processing searches that we discussed earlier:

1. We access the development server environment again, and we will make some further changes to our dashboard. So move into the `views` directory for your Splunk App with the following command:

   cd $SPLUNK_HOME/etc/apps/cell_biology/default/data/ui/views/

2. We move down to line 4 and we are going to add in a separate search for our base search. We open up the search element as we normally would, but we need to set an ID of `baseSearch`:

```
4   <search id="baseSearch">
```

3. We will then set up a query that all our searches in the dashboard will now use. If you look through all our searches, you will notice that they all use the same four search functions as we will add to our new query on the next line:

```
5     <query><![CDATA[ index=main sourcetype=cellsimulation |
      eval data=_raw | rex field=data max_match=0 "(?
      <cells>\@)" | stats count(cells) AS Count by _time ]]>
      </query>
6   </search>
```

4. As we have added three lines here, we need to move down a little further to our first search for the **Zero Cell Count** panel. Here, we will amend our search element to now use the `baseSearch` set up earlier:

```
11      <search base="baseSearch">
```

5. Our query for this panel will now only need to have part of the search to extract zero-value cell counts:

```
12      <query><![CDATA[ | where Count=0 | stats Count |eval
        class=if(Count>1000,"severe","low") ]]>
        </query>
```

6. As you can see, we have simplified the query that needs to be added to our search once we start using the base search that we set up at the start of the dashboard.

7. Now we can move on to the second panel, amend the search element to now use `baseSearch`, and change the query to use the output of `baseSearch`:

```
27      <search base="baseSearch">
28      <query><![CDATA[ | where Count<=10 | stats count ]]>
        </query>
```

8. Move to the third panel and update the search and query elements listed as follows:

```
40      <search base="baseSearch">
41      <query><![CDATA[ | where Count>=20 | stats count
        ]]> </query>
```

9. Let's now make changes to the searches of our final two panels; as you can see, they will be similar to the changes made earlier:

```
55          <search base="baseSearch">
56          <query><![CDATA[ | eval
            description=case(Count<=10, "LOW", Count<=20,
            "MEDIUM", Count>20 , "HIGH") | stats
            count(eval(description="LOW")) as LOW
            count(eval(description="MEDIUM")) as     MEDIUM
            count(eval(description="HIGH")) as HIGH by
            description ]]> </query>
```

10. Finally, we can also change the last search on the dashboard to use `baseSearch`:

```
69      <search base="baseSearch">
70      <query><![CDATA[ | eval
        description=case(Count<=10, "LOW", Count<=20,
        "MEDIUM", Count>20 , "HIGH") | top description ]]>
        </query>
```

11. Save all your changes and refresh your cache. Reload your page, and you should now see that all the searches now load, hopefully in a shorter amount of time. Unfortunately, our example in this instance does not have a large amount of data to search through, but you can imagine delays as our data increases.

Using scheduled reports in dashboards

Post processing searches are not the only way we can speed up the display of data in our Splunk App. We can also use a scheduled report to provide data for the interface we are creating. Using a scheduled report, we also work around some of the limitations that are put in place when using post processing searches, and with large data sets we can run our report once a week and ensure that the data is present before users need to view it.

In our example, we are going to create a new dashboard using a scheduled search. We are hoping to establish that as the generations of cell growth continue, there is a chance that the number of cells that we see will be reduced. We can start by creating our saved search in our Cell Biology Splunk App and we can then create the new dashboard:

1. Log in to your development server and change to the default directory of your Splunk App:

   cd $SPLUNK_HOME/etc/apps/cell_biology/default/

2. We are going to create a new file in this directory, so open up your text editor and create a file named `savedsearches.conf`.

3. You'll be surprised how simple this is. We start by giving our saved search a name that we will use to refer to in our dashboard. In this instance, we will call it `CountGeneration`:

```
1 [CountGeneration]
```

4. The next line will be the schedule for when the search will be run. We will be running it every 5 minutes, which is a little overkill, but once we move our changes into production, we will set it to run daily or weekly:

```
2 cron_schedule = */5 * * * *
```

5. Remember that when setting up the schedule, you need to take into consideration different factors that may effect the delivery of the data. For example, will running the schedule every 5 minutes on a production environment overload the search head and cause an issue with reporting performance?

6. The next few lines will handle how the data will be displayed once the search is run. We are first saying not to allow a timeRangePicker, allowing it instead to be a visualization of raw data, allowing it to be available as a visualization on the search tab, and finally setting it up as an area chart:

```
3 display.general.timeRangePicker.show = 0
4 display.general.type = visualizations
5 display.page.search.tab = visualizations
6 display.visualizations.charting.chart = area
```

7. We can now enable it as a scheduled report, and allow the scheduled search to be set up as part of our Cell Biology Splunk App:

```
7 enableSched = 1
8 request.ui_dispatch_app = cell_biology
```

8. Finally, we can specify the search that will run with the scheduled report:

```
9 search = index=main sourcetype=cellsimulation | eval
  data=_raw | rex field=data max_match=0 "(?<cells>\@)" | rex
  field=_raw "Generation (?<Generation>.*)" | where
  Generation>10 | stats count(cells)    AS Count by
  Generation
```

9. Save the file and then we wait for the scheduled report to run.

When we set up a scheduled report to be displayed in our dashboard, Splunk will choose the most recent report that has been scheduled to run. If no reports have been run, you will see the following warning in your dashboard:

 Warning: saved search not found: "CountGeneration"

We can now set up the dashboard that will display this report:

1. We move into the views directory for our Splunk App so that we can create a new dashboard:

    cd $SPLUNK_HOME/etc/apps/cell_biology/default/data/ui/views/

2. Create a new file named cell_generation.xml, and start setting up the dashboard XML by adding the opening dashboard element and giving the dashboard a label and description:

    ```
    1 <dashboard>
    2   <label>Cell Simulation by Generation</label>
    3   <description>Show a breakdown of live cells through the
      generations</description>
    ```

3. Now create your first row element with a panel, chart, and title element:

    ```
    4   <row>
    5     <panel>
    6       <chart>
    7         <title>Generational Report</title>
    ```

4. Now, when we create our search element, the only thing that we need to do is refer to the scheduled report that we have just created:

    ```
    8         <search ref="CountGeneration">
    ```

5. Now set the type of chart to be an area chart:

    ```
    9           <option name="charting.chart">area</option>
    ```

6. Finally, we can now close off all our elements and save our new dashboard file:

```
10              </search>
11            </chart>
12          </panel>
13        </row>
14 </dashboard>
```

7. We don't really need to do this, but we will also make sure that our navigation is set up to show this new dashboard as well. So move into the navigation directory:

cd $SPLUNK_HOME/etc/apps/cell_biology/default/data/ui/nav/

8. Open the default.xml file, move to the third line in the file, and add the following line:

```
3    <view name="cell_generation" />
```

9. Save all your changes and refresh the Splunk cache. Hopefully, by now, your scheduled report has been run and your dashboard will have something to display:

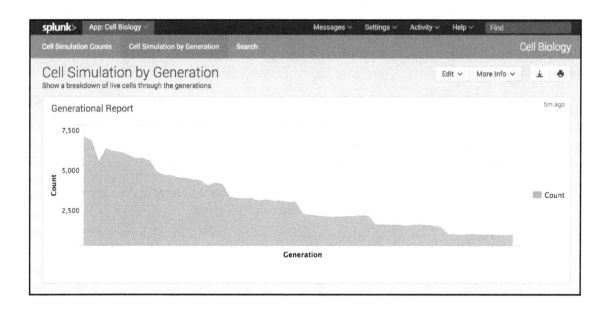

How easy was that! We just set up this cool dashboard in only 14 lines of Simple XML, and the load time was almost instant as Splunk does not need to actually run a search to populate the area chart with data.

> One thing that we will not cover in the book is *Summary indexes* in Splunk. Summary indexes are another good way to speed up the data we display to our users and reports, but it is beyond the scope of this book. Although it is a more advanced feature of Splunk, it is well worth exploring if you are interested in speeding up the data that is presented to your users.

Splunk forms

We have done a lot of work on getting the information that we want to our users, but what if our users want to interact with the data directly? There are default options in Splunk dashboards to allow users to open the visualization in a search page, but if our user does not know how to use the Splunk search interface, this is of little use. With a minor change to the Simple XML we currently have, we can set up our dashboard as a form and allow the user to add input into the way that our visualizations are run and allow them to directly interact with the data.

We will continue to work on our Cell Biology example, and in the rest of this chapter, we will focus on setting up a form that will allow our users to interact with the data. I think it would be interesting to allow our users to choose the value for the number of generations that we can see in the chart that we made in our last example. So we will now create a new dashboard, but this time it will be a form, and set up a drop-down list for users to choose the value:

1. As we have done with a lot of our work, we move into the views directory of our Cell Biology Splunk App:

   cd $SPLUNK_HOME/etc/apps/cell_biology/default/data/ui/views/

2. Create a new file in the views directory called `cell_user_generation.xml`. This time, we are not going to start with the dashboard element. We are creating a form. So–you guessed it–start with the `form` element:

   ```
   1 <form>
   ```

3. The `form` element is similar to a dashboard element but includes some extra features to allow you to set user inputs as needed to gather information from the user. First, however, we will put in a simple label, as we have with our other examples, to explain what we are doing:

```
2    <label>Cell Simulation Defined by User</label>
```

4. As with any form, we need to create a set of fields that the user can enter values into. This is where we use the `fieldset` element in Simple XML. `fieldset` takes a number of values; in our example, we are going to allow the report to `autoRun`, and we are not going to set up a submit button in this instance. We can then use the input element to set up a dropdown menu, with the default value of 10, and also set up the rest of the values that the user can choose from:

```
3    <fieldset autoRun="true" submitButton="false">
4      <input type="dropdown" token="generation_tok">
5        <label>Select a Generation Value</label>
6        <default>10</default>
7        <choice value="5">5</choice>
8        <choice value="10">10</choice>
9        <choice value="15">15</choice>
10        <choice value="20">20</choice>
11        <choice value="25">25</choice>
12        <choice value="30">30</choice>
13      </input>
14    </fieldset>
```

5. In the input element, we have set the token value. In this instance, it is called `generation_tok`. This is how we can change our value in our search to match the selection in the drop-down. In the same way as we would use a variable in other programming languages, when we choose a value in the drop-down, it will be assigned to the token.

6. We can now start setting up our rows and panels in the same way that we would with a normal dashboard, by opening a row, panel, chart, and search element:

```
15    <row>
16      <panel>
17        <chart>
18          <label>Genrational Report Defined by User</label>
19          <search>
```

7. We can now add the token value that we created in our `fieldset` into our search query. As you can see in our statement in the query, we are using the token `generation_tok` value, which is wrapped in two dollar signs ($). This will mean that the value that we chose from the drop-down menu will be assigned to this value in the search query:

```
20              <query> <![CDATA[
                index=main sourcetype=cellsimulation
                | eval data=_raw
                | rex field=data max_match=0 "(?<cells>\@)"
                | rex field=_raw "Generation (?<Generation>.*)"
                | where Generation>$generation_tok$
                | stats count(cells) AS Count by Generation ]]>
                </query>
```

8. We can now close off the search element and we will use an option for our chart element to set it this time as a line graph:

```
21              </search>
22              <option name="charting.chart">line</option>
```

9. We can now close off our chart, panel, row, and form elements to finish our the user interface:

```
23          </chart>
24        </panel>
25      </row>
26 </form>
```

10. We save the new file that we have created, and while we are in working on our development environment, we will also set up the navigation for this page so that our users will be able to access it from the Splunk App. You will need to move into the navigation or `nav` directory:

cd $SPLUNK_HOME/etc/apps/cell_biology/default/data/ui/nav/

11. Open the `default.xml` file. Move down to the fourth line and add the following line:

```
4    <view name="cell_user_generation" />
```

12. We save the file, refresh the Splunk cache again, and open up the new form that we have created:

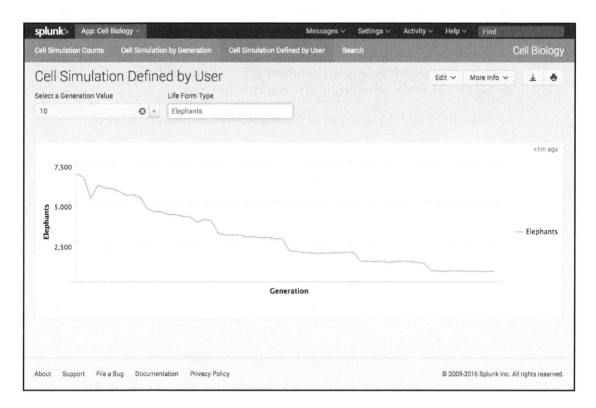

The chart that we have created is not anything that we hadn't seen before. Our last example is almost exactly the same. In this instance though, we have a nice drop-down menu by which the user can now change the value of the number of generations that get presented in our line graph.

Our fieldset element is not limited to one type or only one entry point. We can add multiple fields to our form by adding a new input value into the fieldset element. We will keep going with our current form. I was thinking, we are currently counting cells in our simulation, but what if we want to give our users the option enter in whatever type of simulation they are performing? Maybe they are simulating elephant behavior in a zoo enclosure, so now we can set up a text box to allow our users to define anything they want:

1. We access our development environment again and move to the views directory so that we can make some changes to our current form:

   cd $SPLUNK_HOME/etc/apps/cell_biology/default/data/ui/views/

2. Open up the `cell_user_generation.xml` file with your text editor so that you can add some extra user input fields.

3. We closed off our drop-down input type at line 13 in our previous work. Add four new lines after this and we will set up a text box field. We start by opening up our `input` element, specifying the type, and also setting up the token value name:

   ```
   14     <input type="text" token="cell_tok">
   ```

4. Next, set up a lable for our text box so our users will know what the text box is for:

   ```
   15     <label>Life Form Type</label>
   ```

5. We have been counting cells in our previous examples, so we can add this as a default value. We can then close off our input value and we have successfully added our text box:

   ```
   16     <default>Cells</default>
   17     </input>
   ```

6. We now need to let our search query know that it needs to use the new token that we have created for our text input. We move down to our search query and change it to the following line so that our `stats` function will now use the new `cell_tok` token:

```
24    <query> <![CDATA[
      index=main sourcetype=cellsimulation
      | eval data=_raw
      | rex field=data max_match=0 "(?<cells>\@)"
      | rex field=_raw "Generation (?<Generation>.*)"
      | where Generation>$generation_tok$
      | stats count(cells) AS $cell_tok$ by Generation ]]>
      </query>
```

7. Save the changes you have made and reload the Splunk Cache. Log in to the web interface again and access your form. You should see a new textbox with the label of **Life Form Type** and it should have the default entry of `cells`.

8. We can test our changes now that we have this new feature in our example. I am going to see if I can enter the value of `Elephants`, and hopefully when I hit *Enter*, the graph should be loaded and count elephants instead of cells.

More advanced form examples

I want to take a moment to introduce checkboxes to our example. The feature is a fairly recent addition to SimpleXML, but it can be a little confusing how to actually implement the feature in a form, and that is why I am describing it as an advanced form example. When checkboxes are working properly though, it can be a nice addition as it allows your users to specify the values they want and compare when needed.

This is where we will change our example from a drop-down menu to checkboxes, which will allow the user to not only display the generation value they need but also compare between multiple generations.

Access your development server again. We are going to make quite a few changes to the `cell_user_generation.xml` form that we created earlier:

1. Start by accessing the development environment. Move into the views directory and open the `cell_user_generation.xml` file with your text editor.

2. Move down to line 4, where we define the type input, and change the line to the following. This will change the input type to a checkbox and make sure that each time we change the selection, a new search will be run:

```
4       <input type="checkbox" token="generation_tok"
        searchWhenChanged="true">
```

3. The good thing about the change we have just made is that we do not need to change any of the default or choice elements as we are going to keep them the same. But this is where things get a little difficult.

4. Move down to line 13, where we closed off our input element previously, and instead we want to add the following five lines of code:

```
13      <prefix>(</prefix>
14      <suffix>)</suffix>
15      <valuePrefix>Generation="</valuePrefix>
16      <valueSuffix>"</valueSuffix>
17      <delimiter> OR </delimiter>
```

5. This code is specifying how our token will now be set up. The prefix and suffix describe how the token will start and finish; in our code, we have it enclosed in brackets. The `valuePrefix` is what will come before the value that we select. The `valueSuffix` will be what comes after our value. And finally, as we are chaining multiple values together, we need to use the delimiter of OR.

6. For example, if we select 5 and 30, our token will be the value of:

```
(Generation="5" OR Generation="30")
```

7. Now that we have a new token value, we need to add this to our search query. Move down to the query that is now on line 29 and replace it with the following as our `where` function will now change to use the new token:

```
29      <query> <![CDATA[
        index=main sourcetype=cellsimulation
        | eval data=_raw
        | rex field=data max_match=0 "(?<cells>\@)"
        | rex field=_raw "Generation (?<Generation>.*)"
        | where $generation_tok$
        |       timechart span=1h count(cells) AS $cell_tok$ by
        Generation ]]> </query>
```

8. Save the changes to your form and reload the Splunk cache. Open up the form and you should now see something similar to the following screenshot:

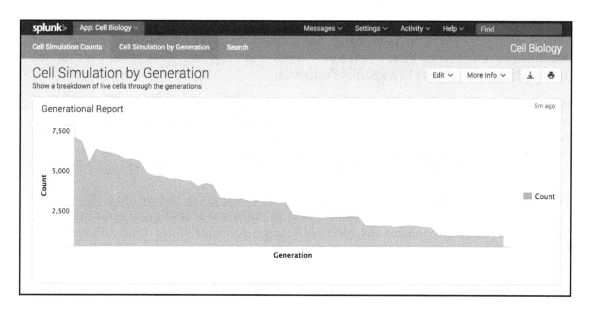

If everything goes as planned, the form should now be displaying five separate checkboxes instead of the drop-down menu. The user can make as many selections as they want and the following line chart will then load with each selection. At the bottom-left corner of the chart, there is a magnifying class icon that allows you to *Open in Search*. If you click on this, you will be able to see the exact search query that is being used, including the checkbox values that we have provided:

```
index=main sourcetype=cellsimulation | eval data=_raw | rex field=data
max_match=0 "(?<cells>\@)" | rex field=_raw "Generation (?<Generation>.*)"
| where (Generation="5" OR Generation="15" OR Generation="30") | timechart
span=1h count(cells) AS Cells by Generation
```

Drilldown of data within Splunk

We just used the magnifying glass icon at the bottom left of the chart, which is a type of drilldown to allow users to look further into the data presented by the dashboard or form. We have used some of the basic options already, and our panels will also come with the default setting to view the data in search, but we can customize the behavior of our drilldown information further. When a user clicks on a value in a visualization, we can use that value to send the user to a specific destination.

With the examples that we have been using so far, the only time that we have been working with drilldown in Simple XML is when we are setting chart options to see if they are available in our panel or which cell they will be mapped to. Drilldowns have their own element available to use in Simple XML, which is named drilldown and allows us to specifically define the behavior that takes place when a user clicks on a relevant field.

The form that we created as part of our example is looking good, but we are going to add an extra table to the bottom so that we can see how to make use of configuring our drilldown data. Access your development environment, change into your views directory, and get your text editor to make some changes to the `cell_user_generation.xml` file:

1. Move down to the bottom of the file, and we are going to set up another table showing the HIGH, MEDIUM and LOW values of our cell simulations. We can start by opening row, panel, table and title elements:

```
35    <row>
36      <panel>
37        <table>
38          <title>Drilldown for More Information</title>
```

2. Now we set up our search and query:

```
39          <search>
40            <query> <![CDATA[
              index=main sourcetype=cellsimulation | eval
              data=_raw
              | rex field=data max_match=0 "(?<cells>\@)"
              | stats count(cells) AS Count by _time
              | eval description=case(Count<=10,"LOW",
              Count<=20, "MEDIUM", Count>20 , "HIGH")
              | top description ]]> </query>
41          </search>
```

3. This is where things start to get a little different. If we want to make a change to the way a drilldown works, we open up a drilldown element. This is where we can change the way our drilldown will work. The link target is _blank as we are using our Splunk App, and we then specify the actual form, called cell_target, that we are going to create:

```
42          <drilldown>
43            <link target="_blank">
44              /app/cell_biology/cell_target?
                form.src_cell_range=$row.description$
```

4. The last value of $row.description$ is the token that we are going to feed into our next form. It is basically saying that we will be using the field in the row that we click, under the description column.

5. Now close off your link and description elements:

```
45            </link>
46          </drilldown>
```

6. Finally, we want to set the drilldown option of row:

```
47          <option name="drilldown">row</option>
```

7. We can now close off our table, panel, row and form elements:

```
48          </table>
49        </panel>
50      </row>
51  </form>
```

8. If you save your changes and reload the Splunk cache, your page will load with the new table at the bottom of the page. If you click on the values in the table though, a new page will be loaded with the **Page Not Found** error. To fix this, we can create the new form that we want to load.

The cool thing about drilldowns is that we don't have to limit ourselves to Splunk App dashboards and web pages. If we wanted to, we could link our chart to the Wikipedia page for a description of Conway's Game of Life with the following elements:

```
<drilldown>
  <link>
    https://en.wikipedia.org/wiki/Conway%27s_Game_of_Life
  </link>
</drilldown>
```

You can even pass your tokens to external web pages. In this instance, we will continue to set up our drilldown to direct us to a new form that we are now going to create.

If we had the default drilldown values set up, clicking on the values in the table would open a new search screen, with a table of results. Which is good, but in this situation, we want to display the same search values in a column chart:

1. We should still be in our `views` directory from our last changes. Open up a new file called `cell_target.xml` as we discussed earlier when setting up the drilldown link.

2. It should be able to accept the token that we created previously in our drilldown configuration, so we will need to create a form. Open up the form element, add a label, and add a `fieldset` element:

```
1 <form>
2   <label>Cell Ranges (Target Form)</label>
3   <fieldset submitButton="false" autoRun="true">
```

3. Add a text input that will accept the token that we created earlier as `src_cell_range`. We can also label:

```
4       <input type="text" token="src_cell_range"
        searchWhenChanged="true">
5         <label>Range Type</label>
6       </input>
7   </fieldset>
```

4. We can now set up our chart as we normally would with row, panel, chart, and title elements:

```
8    <row>
9      <panel>
10        <chart>
11          <title>Cell Range Details</title>
```

5. When we set up our search element, our query will use the `src_cell_range` token that we first created in our drilldown configuration, and now passed to our new form:

```
12        <search>
13          <query> <![CDATA[
          index=main sourcetype=cellsimulation | eval
          data=_raw
          | rex field=data max_match=0 "(?<cells>\@)"
          | stats count(cells) AS Count by _time
          | eval description=case(Count<=10,"LOW",
          Count<=20, "MEDIUM", Count>20 , "HIGH")
          | where description="$src_cell_range$"
          | timechart span=1hour count by description ]]>
          </query>
14        </search>
```

6. As we mentioned earlier, we also want to display our data as a column chart:

```
15        <option name="charting.chart">column</option>
```

7. All we now need to do is close off our chart, panel, row, and form elements to finish our form:

```
16        </chart>
17      </panel>
18    </row>
19 </form>
```

8. Save the new file that we created, reload the Splunk cache, and open our original **Cell Simulation Defined by User** form. Now when we click on the values of the table, the new form that we created displaying our column chart should now be opened in a new browser window:

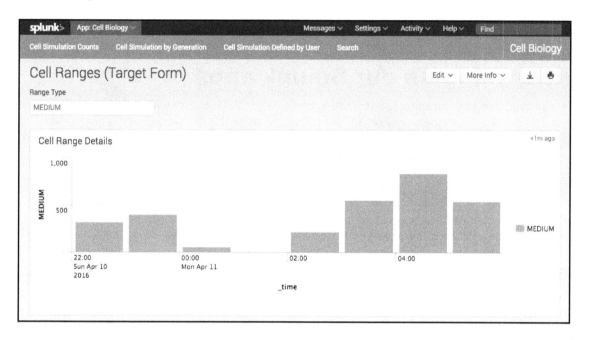

We have moved through things pretty quickly here, but if you need to read up a little further on drilldown configurations in your Simple XML, see the following link for further information:

```
http://docs.splunk.com/Documentation/Splunk/latest/Viz/Dynamicdrilldownindas
hboardsandforms
```

Packaging up our Splunk apps

So far, we have been doing a lot of work with Git and GitHub in tracking our changes and controlling our development process. We have also used it as a method of deploying our Splunk App across our development, test, and production environments. Git is a great way to do this, and we should continue to work this way, especially in the development environment, but when it comes to deploying across production environments, we should start to look at packaging our Splunk App in the approved Splunkpackage format.

This is where we can package our application up to be installed and deployed onto a production server. And if you are ever wanting to have your Splunk App hosted as a certified Splunk App available to the general public and possibly available for purchase, you will need to start packaging up your Splunk App.

Our Cell Biology Splunk App has come a long way, but we will now finish off the final steps to get it ready for our production deployment. We should have thoroughly tested the Splunk App across development and test environments, and all our changes should also be committed and merged to our master branch in GitHub, ready to be packaged up:

1. We start by logging in to an environment that has the master code of our Splunk App checked out and working. We move to our Cell Biology Splunk App and we can start to make preparations for our package:

    ```
    cd $SPLUNK_HOME/etc/apps/cell_biology/
    ```

2. In the previous chapter, we started working with the app.conf file that is located in the default directory of our Splunk App. If you created the app using either the Splunk App builder or the command line, the app.conf file will be created for you. The main things you need to worry about for your first package are setting the ui values to make sure that your Splunk App is visible and has a valid label, and the launcher details, which contain the version, author, and description:

    ```
    8 [ui]
    9 is_visible = true
    ```

```
10 label = Cell Biology
11
12 [launcher]
13 author = <your name>
14 description = <add a description>
15 version = 1.0
```

3. For a full breakdown an explanation of all the options available for the app.conf file, check out the following documentation from Splunk: http://docs.splunk.com/Documentation/Splunk/latest/AdvancedDev/PackageApp.

4. We have not been adding scripts to our Splunk App, but if you have to, make sure that all the relevant scripts that your Splunk App needs to function are included in the bin directory of the app.

5. This is the tricky part. Your Splunk App may be using searches, reports, views, navigation, and configuration files that are not located in the current Splunk App directory. You need to make sure that all of these values are now in your Splunk App default directory. The main directory you will need to check is the local directory of your Splunk App. For example, if you have a savedsearches.conf file that your Splunk App uses, you will need to copy the relevant file or specific saved search to your default directory.

6. If you are releasing your Splunk App to other users and need to provide documentation, especially for installation, configuration and usage, place a README.txt file in the Splunk App directory.

7. We have been using Git to track our changes and use during our development process, but we do not need to include all the specific Git files as part of our package, so we remove any Git files from our Splunk App:

   rm -rf $SPLUNK_HOME/etc/apps/cell_biology/.git

8. Finally, make sure that if you have any configurations in your Splunk App that require authentication or account names to be provided (for example, connecting to a network device to read logs), these are removed.

9. It's now time to tar and zip up our Splunk app:

   tar zcvf cell_biology.tar.gz
   $SPLUNK_HOME/etc/apps/cell_biology/*

10. We could simply use this file created to deploy to our production environment. The Splunkbase does require that all Splunk Apps use the `.spl` file extension, so we will perform this change make sure that it is also Splunkbase legal:

```
cd  $SPLUNK_HOME/etc/apps/
mv cell_biology.tar.gz cell_biology.spl
```

11. Before deploying your Splunk App on a production environment, you should verify that your installation works on a clean Splunk environment, separate from the one that you created the package on to make sure that it deploys correctly and the basic functionality works correctly. You may remember that the Manage Apps screen on the Splunk Web interface allows you to install a Splunk App from a file. Alternatively, you can use a command directly on the server as long as you have your new package transferred over to it:

```
$SPLUNK_HOME/bin/splunk install app cell_biology.spl
```

As you can see, the packaging up of the Splunk App is straightforward, but you do need to make sure that any dependencies have been accounted for to ensure that it works as a standalone Splunk App on any server that you deploy it to.

Packaging our Cell Biology Splunk App is a great way to bring our development of this example to a conclusion. Over the past two chapters, we have moved from some simple lines of code to a fully functional data-reporting tool. Our users are able to view, compare and interact with the data by using both dashboards and forms. We have worked to ensure that our searches have been optimized for speed and ensure as much as possible the users are not waiting for data to load by utilizing scheduled searches and post processing searches. We have also developed and extended our knowledge of Simple XML, JavaScript, and CSS, and finally, we have a fully packaged Splunk App that can quite easily be certified, added to the Splunkbase, and distributed to other Splunkenvironments, ready for deployment directly on their systems. Take two minutes to be content with what you have achieved, but get excited because there is still a lot more to come.

Summary

In this chapter, we did a lot of work to enhance the user experience of our Splunk App by working within Simple XML to speed up the delivery of our charts and visualizations to our users. We introduced post processing searches to ensure that we are not wasting the processing power of our Splunk Search server. We were able to configure our example to ensure that only one main search is performed, with the data then feeding into the rest of our panels on the dashboard. We also set up a scheduled search to run at a specific time so that our data would be available to present in our visualizations before they are loaded, speeding up the process even further.

We started working with the form element of our Simple XML code to allow users to interact directly with the data presented in their Splunk Apps via the use of fields. We also looked at search drilldowns and customized them further to guide the user to specific searches that they may find more useful. Finally, we packaged up our Cell Biology Splunk App to allow it to be distributed directly to all our Splunkenvironments via the standard installation interface.

In our next chapter, we are going to continue our momentum and develop our knowledge even further by moving from Simple XML to HTML dashboards. We are going to discuss the intricacies of why we would want to use HTML, show you how to create your first HTML dashboard, and provide a detailed explanation of the parts of the HTML code. We are also going to introduce our new example Splunk App, which works with stock market data, where we will learn how to change and manipulate the dashboard elements and explain how searches will work once you have moved to HTML.

6
Moving from Simple XML to HTML

We are about to take our coding skills to the next level. Just as we did when we moved from using the Splunk Web Interface and started creating and editing our Splunk Apps in Simple XML, we increased functionality of what we are providing to our users and were able to provide a cleaner and more polished user interface. Well, this is what we are going to be doing by now, moving from Simple XML to HTML.

By moving our Splunk App to HTML from Simple XML, we allow our code to be enhanced further by accessing specific HTML, CSS, and JavaScript functionality that would not be available to us by only using Simple XML. Although we can add both CSS and JavaScript to our Simple XML code, we are still limited in how far we can go. For example, moving to HTML allows us to then implement ARIA into our dashboards to improve accessibility for people with disabilities who may be wanting to work with our dashboards and data.

We could settle with what we have learned and implemented with Simple XML, but why stop there? This is where we are going to start to customize our reports and visualizations even further, by using HTML dashboards, while we introduce our new example Splunk App that will draw on stock market data.

In this chapter we will:

- Introducing HTML dashboards and explain how to convert your Simple XML dashboards to HTML
- Discussing some of the benefits of using HTML over Simple XML
- Editing HTML dashboards with the Splunk Code Editor
- Providing a detailed explanation of the code involved in producing an HTML dashboard.

- Discussing how to customize, change, and configure the code to our liking.
- Providing an explanation of how Splunk searches now work in HTML dashboards
- Exploring the setting up of a Splunk App template to help fast-track our code development.

If you don't have a lot of experience with HTML, CSS, or JavaScript, don't worry. We are going to take things pretty easy and step through the code as we have been in previous chapters, with lots of examples and descriptions of the code and changes we are making.

Moving forward by taking a step back

We are going to start our work with HTML by setting up another Simple XML Splunk App. It sounds like we are taking a step back, but this will firstly reinforce some of the information we have learned so far, introduce the new example Splunk App that we are going to create, and hopefully allow us to move even faster when we start working with HTML code.

As we discussed in our first chapter, we are going to use data from the Yahoo! Finance API, which provides Stock Market data for companies listed on the stock exchange. We can use the API provided by Yahoo! to download the data we need. For our example, we can use as many companies as we like, but I am going to get both Yahoo! and Splunk company stock market data. If you have not used the API before, all you need to do is work out the URL commands specific for the API, place this URL in a web browser, or use the curl command from your server.

The two URLs that I used to get my data were as follows:

- Yahoo!:
  http://ichart.finance.yahoo.com/table.csv?s=YHOO&d=0&e=1&f=2016&g=d&a=1&b=0&c=2015&ignore=.csv
- Splunk: `http://ichart.finance.yahoo.com/table.csv?s=SPLK&d=0&e=1&f=2016&g=d&a=1&b=0&c=2015&ignore=.csv`

Although the URL we created to extract our data does look a little complex, a breakdown of each of the command options is provided as follows:

- `s`: Company symbol (Yahoo!=YHOO, Splunk=SPLK)
- `d`: To month -1
- `e`: To day

- f: To year
- g: Set up of date (d for day, m for month, y for yearly)
- a: From month -1
- b: From day (two digits)
- c: From year

Copies of the stock market data that we are using as part of this example will be available as part of the chapter download, but if you need a more detailed explanation of the options for using the API, please go to the Yahoo Finance site at the following link: `https://finance.yahoo.com/`.

When I indexed the data into my Splunk environment, I created a source type specific for the data, called `stockcsv`. The difference between this source type and the normal CSV source type is as follows:

- Timestamp format: `%Y-%m-%d`
- Timestamp field: `Date`

This change will make it easier to produce time-based reports because the time will not be set as the time the data was indexed and will be set as the Date in the CSV file.

Now that we have all our formalities out of the way, we can set up our new Splunk App and a basic dashboard. As we discussed in earlier chapters, it is best to create our Splunk App from the web interface, so this is where we will start:

1. When presented with the form to create a new Splunk App, use the following details to create our new examples.
2. From the **Apps** management screen, click on the **Create app** button.
3. Log on to your development Splunk environment from the web interface, and from the welcome screen, click on the **Manage Apps** icon, which is the cog next to the word Apps at the top left of the screen:
   - **Name:** `Stock Market`
   - **Folder Name**: `stock_market`
   - **Version**: `0.1`
   - **Author**: Enter your name
   - **Description**: Enter a description
   - **Template**: `barebones`

4. Once you are happy with the entries you have made in your form, click on the **Save** button to create the new Splunk App. Remember to set up a new repository in GitHub and continue to add your code to the repository.

We are going to start by creating a Simple XML dashboard, providing a comparison between our two data samples. You should almost be an expert at this by now, but log in to the development server and we will get started:

1. We move into our `views` directory within our new Splunk App:

   cd $SPLUNK_HOME/etc/apps/stock_market/default/data/ui/views/

2. We will create an overview page to be displayed by default when we open the Stock Market Splunk App. Open a new file called `overview.xml` with your text editor and start by opening your dashboard element and giving your new dashboard a label:

   ```
   1 <dashboard>
   2   <label>Stock Market Historical Overview</label>
   ```

3. Now open the row, panel, and chart elements:

   ```
   3   <row>
   4     <panel>
   5       <chart>
   ```

4. Give your chart a title and open a search element ready for your query:

   ```
   6         <title>Historical Overview of Stock Value</title>
   7         <search>
   ```

5. The query for the dashboard will be basic but should give us a comparison between the different close values of the stock we have indexed in our environment:

   ```
   8   <query> <![CDATA[ sourcetype="stockcsv"
      | chart values(Close) by Date source ]]> </query>
   ```

6. We only want the data for the last calendar year, so we set up the element that will specify the earliest date for the search, and then we can close off the search element:

```
9        <earliest>-1y@y</earliest>
10       </search>
```

7. We set up our chart option to display a line chart, and we can then close the remaining elements:

```
11              <option name="charting.chart">line</option>
12           </chart>
13         </panel>
14      </row>
15  </dashboard>
```

8. Save the new file. Before we test our new dashboard, let's make sure it is displayed in our menu across the top of the screen of our app and is also displayed by default when we open our Splunk App.

9. Move to the nav directory so that we can configure our navigation for our Splunk App:

cd $SPLUNK_HOME/etc/apps/stock_market/default/data/ui/nav/

10. Open up the default.xml file with a text editor. We are going to remove most of the menu options and provide the new dashboard that we have created, and the only other item that will display at the top of the screen will be the search page:

```
1 <nav search_view="search" color="#65A637">
2   <view name="overview" default='true' />
3   <view name="search" />
4 </nav>
```

11. We save the file and refresh Splunk's cache so that our changes will take effect. If all goes as planned, we should have a page similar to the following screenshot, where we have the closing values of our stock being compared to each other over time:

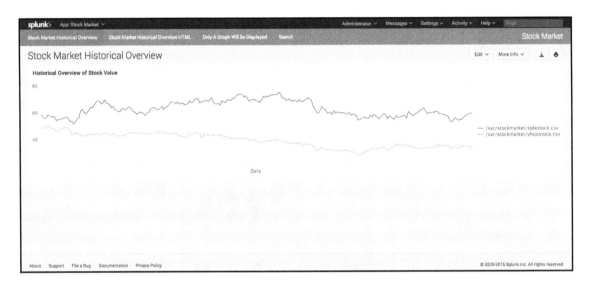

This is where things start to get a little more interesting. By creating a new Simple XML dashboard, we can now use the Splunk Web Interface to convert this dashboard from Simple XML to an HTML dashboard. In the next few pages, we will convert it to a HTML dashboard, use the Splunk HTML Code Editor to view the changes we have made, and then step through the code and explain what each part of the code does. There is a lot to cover, so let's get started.

Converting your Simple XML code to HTML

Splunk provides an easy way for you to get started with HTML dashboards by converting your original Simple XML into HTML code. We've just created our new Stock Market Splunk App, so we will get started by converting our Overview dashboard to HTML:

1. Log in to the web interface for your development Splunk environment and access the Stock Market Splunk App. Our overview dashboard should be loading as the default page.

2. Click on the **Edit** drop-down menu near the top right of the dashboard and select **Convert to HTML**.

3. You will be presented with the following form. Select the default values for the **Title** and **ID** of the dashboard, and make sure that **Create New** is selected for the dashboard and **Shared** is set as **Permissions**.

4. You don't need to set a **Description**, but when you are happy with your selections, click on the **Create Dashboard** button.

After you've created the new HTML dashboard, you will be presented with the option to view the dashboard in the web interface or in the HTML editor. Load up the page in the web interface and you will notice that your dashboard will look exactly the same. There are some minor changes that have been made.

The first will be that the title of the dashboard is now **Stock Market Historical Overview HTML**, as we accepted the default that the previous form gave us. You also won't have the option of **Export to PDF** near the top right of the dashboard. The last main difference you will notice is that you are a lot more limited with the options presented in the **Edit** menu. Once you convert a dashboard to HTML, you will no longer be able to use the Splunk Web Interface to make changes to HTML dashboards. If you want to make changes to your dashboard once it is converted to HTML, you will only be able to do this through the code itself.

The Splunk HTML Code Editor

When we first started working with Simple XML, we saw that Splunk provides a Code Editor as part of the web interface. The Splunk Code Editor also allows you to work with your HTML code in exactly the same way. As we discussed a little earlier, HTML dashboards are now limited in the options provided by the **Edit** menu near the top-right corner of the dashboard. It does offer the option to Edit Source, which will open your HTML source code in the Splunk HTML Code Editor. Hopefully, it will look similar to the following screenshot:

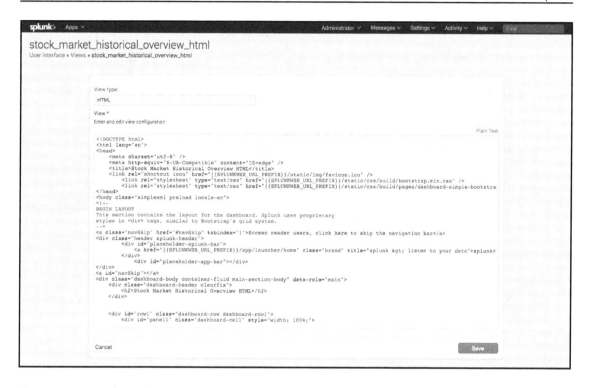

As you can see from the preceding screenshot, the editor is basic but it does provide us with a description of the code type, coloring and indentation of the code, and basic error checking of the code, hopefully pointing out any issues when we try to save any changes. If you want to use your own text editor or IDE, the location of the file will be similar to your Simple XML dashboards and forms. As we have created this HTML dashboard via the web interface, it will be in the local directory of our Splunk App directory. This time though, instead of being in the `views` directory, it will be in the `html` directory. If you want to open the HTML file with your text editor, you would do so by going to the following directory location on your server:

```
$SPLUNK_HOME/etc/apps/stock_market/local/data/ui/html/
```

Stepping through the HTML dashboard code

I am sure you have noticed that the code is looking a lot different when it is in HTML form. When we created this dashboard, we used 15 lines of Simple XML code, and now in HTML, it is closer to 300 lines of code. Let's start stepping through the code we have created and give you a breakdown of what each of the sections does.

As we walk through the code, you will notice that there are five distinct sections of it:

- HTML metadata and style sheets, where we can set up the metadata for the page and load style sheets.
- HTML layout code is where we set up the `div` containers and call search and chart elements from the further sections in the code.
- JavaScript and Tokens, where the JavaScript libraries are loaded. This is also where the tokens for the dashboards are set up.
- Search managers is the area where we set up the search queries that are used for the charts and visualizations in our dashboard.
- Visual element details is where we specify the visual elements that are then used in the div containers earlier in the code.

So let's take a closer look.

There is a lot of code that we need to cover here, so we will pass over some of the code and explicitly not show it in the following breakdown. We will do our best to point this out though.

```
1  <!DOCTYPE html>
2  <html lang="en">
3  <head>
4      <meta charset="utf-8" />
5      <meta http-equiv="X-UA-Compatible" content="IE=edge" />
6      <title>Stock Market Historical Overview HTML | Splunk</title>
```

If you are familiar with HTML, this is where we load up our HTML metadata and specify the languages, character set, and title of the page, all of which are contained within the head HTML elements:

```
7      <link rel="shortcut icon" href="
       {{SPLUNKWEB_URL_PREFIX}}/static/img/favicon.ico" />
8      <link rel="stylesheet" type="text/css" href="/en-
       US/static/@264376/css/build/bootstrap.min.css" />
9      <link rel="stylesheet" type="text/css" href="/en-
       US/static/@264376/css/build/pages/dashboard-simple-
       bootstrap.min.css" />
10     <!--[if IE 7]><link rel="stylesheet" href="
       {{SPLUNKWEB_URL_PREFIX}}/static/css/sprites-ie7.css" /><!
       [endif]-->
11  </head>
```

We then specify the style sheets that we are going to use as part of our page. You can see that we are using the Bootstrap CSS, which is part of our Splunk installation. If you have not used Bootstrap before, it is a common framework for creating websites and web applications. It is a free collection of HTML and CSS-based design templates for setting up forms, buttons, and other interface components. If you wanted to define your own style sheets, you would place it in the preceding section of code. If you are familiar with CSS, you would have most likely faced issues with specificity, so ensure that any user-defined style sheets are placed after the imported style sheets:

```
12 <body class="simplexml preload locale-en">
18 <a class="navSkip" href="#navSkip" tabindex="1">Screen reader
   users, click here to skip the navigation bar</a>
```

Our body element opens up the dashboard layout section of our code, and as you can see, it uses the simplexml class to help set up the page. The preceding lines also provide users who are not using a web browser, specifically a screen reader, to skip the navigation and menu options:

```
19 <div class="header splunk-header">
20       <div id="placeholder-splunk-bar">
21           <a href="{{SPLUNKWEB_URL_PREFIX}}/app/launcher/home"
             class="brand" title="splunk &gt; listen to your
             data">splunk<strong>&gt;</strong></a>
22       </div>
23           <div id="placeholder-app-bar"></div>
24   </div>
25 <a id="navSkip"></a>
```

The remaining code sets up a div element to contain the Splunk application header, brand icon, and the Splunk administration menu at the top right of the screen. It then adds the Splunk App navigation that you have set up as part of your code within the nav file system of your code, and would look similar to this image:

Our layout code then sets up our dashboard header with our dashboard Heading 2 elements, and this will also include the **Edit**, **More Info**, and **Printing** menus:

```
26 <div class="dashboard-body container-fluid main-section-body"
   data-role="main">
27     <div class="dashboard-header clearfix">
28         <h2>Stock Market Historical Overview HTML</h2>
29     </div>
```

We can now see that the `div` container elements are setting up the layout sections of the dashboard with familiar identification names such as row and panel, and the class values are self-explanatory, such as `dashboard-row`, `dashboard-cell`, and `dashboard-panel`:

```
32      <div id="row1" class="dashboard-row dashboard-row1">
33          <div id="panel1" class="dashboard-cell" style="width:
            100%;">
34              <div class="dashboard-panel clearfix">
```

Our code then provides the HTML for the chart visualization and the `element1` identifier refers to the chart that will be set up further down in the code:

```
36              <div class="panel-element-row">
37                  <div id="element1" class="dashboard-element
                    chart" style="width: 100%">
38                      <div class="panel-head">
39                      <h3>Historical Overview of Stock
                          Value</h3>
40                      </div>
41                      <div class="panel-body"></div>
```

We then see all our div elements closed off before we get to the final class of the HTML layout, where we show the `footer` class:

```
48 <div class="footer"></div>
```

We now move into the JavaScript section of the code. The first task that the JavaScript takes care of is setting up all the JavaScript library files and specifying the locations that are on your Splunk server:

```
54 <script src="{{SPLUNKWEB_URL_PREFIX}}/config?autoload=1">
   </script>
55 <script src="{{SPLUNKWEB_URL_PREFIX}}/static/js/i18n.js">
   </script>
56 <script src="{{SPLUNKWEB_URL_PREFIX}}/i18ncatalog?autoload=1">
   </script>
57 <script src="
   {{SPLUNKWEB_URL_PREFIX}}
   /static/js/build/simplexml.min/config.js"></script>
58 <script type="text/javascript">
```

The require configuration creates the system's `baseURL` to point to the JavaScript libraries that we will shortly be loading:

```
59 require.config({
60      baseUrl: "{{SPLUNKWEB_URL_PREFIX}}/static/js",
61      waitSeconds: 0 // Disable require.js load timeout
62 });
```

We then see a long list of libraries that are being used as part of the HTML dashboard. The require function maps the library and modules into variable names. We have cut down the list that we have documented here to speed up our discussion:

```
75 require([
76      "splunkjs/mvc",
77      "splunkjs/mvc/utils",
78      "splunkjs/mvc/tokenutils",
79      "underscore",
80      "jquery",
. . .
109     ],
110     function(
111         mvc,
112         utils,
113         TokenUtils,
114         _,
115         $,
116         DashboardController,
. . .
145         ) {
```

In the preceding code, each of the variables maps directly to the libraries. If you are planning to make changes to these lists and add your own custom libraries, you need to make sure that you don't mix up the order of the mapping. Otherwise, your libraries will not load, or even worse, load under a different variable name.

The next 50 lines of code initialize token values that the dashboard is working with. We have used tokens before to enhance our Simple XML forms, and the code is setting up our tokens, so the search managers and views can share the data values between them as we did with our forms. The way the token code works is a more advanced topic, and although you can manipulate the code and change the way tokens work, it is best to not make any changes and leave it as it is.

The next section of code refers to the search managers where we can define and manipulate our searches that are taking place as part of our dashboard. The properties that are defined can be changed and manipulated when needed; for example, the earliest and latest times can be changed and the search property specifically defines the search query being run. In our example, we have only set up a basic search, but if we also included scheduled reports or postprocessing searches, they would be implemented in the search managers section:

```
195        var search1 = new SearchManager({
196            "id": "search1",
197            "status_buckets": 0,
198            "earliest_time": "-1y@y",
199            "search": "sourcetype="stockcsv" | chart
               values(Close) by Date source",
200            "latest_time": "$latest$",
201            "cancelOnUnload": true,
202            "app": utils.getCurrentApp(),
203            "auto_cancel": 90,
204            "preview": true,
205            "runWhenTimeIsUndefined": false
206        }, {tokens: true, tokenNamespace: "submitted"});
```

In our HTML layout section of the code, we used div elements to display the header and footer elements on our dashboard. The following code allows us to see the specified properties that have been used to generate the header and footer details provided to the user:

```
214        new HeaderView({
215            id: 'header',
216            section: 'dashboards',
217            el: $('.header'),
218            acceleratedAppNav: true,
219            useSessionStorageCache: true,
220            splunkbar: true,
221            appbar: true,
222            litebar: false,
223        }, {tokens: true}).render();
224
225        new FooterView({
226            id: 'footer',
227            el: $('.footer')
228        }, {tokens: true}).render();
```

The preceding code gives a clear breakdown of the specific elements in the header and footer of the dashboard we are displaying. Although there is not much to customize, the properties are self-explanatory.

The code then moves on to perform a similar setup of the dashboard elements that we also used in our layout:

```
235            new Dashboard({
236                id: 'dashboard',
237                el: $('.dashboard-body'),
238                showTitle: true,
239                editable: true
240            }, {tokens: true}).render();
```

It doesn't look like much, but we then specify the code for the chart taking place in our dashboard. In the HTML layout, we used the element1 ID, which is being defined next as a line chart using the search1 search that was set up as part of the search managers section:

```
247            var element1 = new ChartElement({
248                "id": "element1",
249                "charting.chart": "line",
250                "resizable": true,
251                "managerid": "search1",
252                "el": $('#element1')
253            }, {tokens: true, tokenNamespace:
               "submitted"}).render();
```

As we can see in the comment, the code then submits any token values that need to be submitted, specifically in our example we are seeing the earliest and latest tokens that will then be able to be used throughout the dashboard:

```
257            // Initialize time tokens to default
258            if (!defaultTokenModel.has('earliest') &&
               !defaultTokenModel.has('latest')) {
259                defaultTokenModel.set({ earliest: '0', latest: '' });
260            }
261
262            submitTokens();
```

The code that has been implemented and set up as part of converting our Simple XML dashboard to HTML is then closed off and ready for us to render.

Why convert to HTML?

There seems to be a lot of code that we have created when we converted our dashboard from Simple XML, and it is probably about now when you are asking if it is worth the effort to actually perform this change. Well, there are a few good reasons you would want to move your dashboards to HTML:

- **Customization**: Even though Simple XML has come a long way, there are still some things you simply cannot do. Just as we found that we were able to create dashboard quicker and with more features when we moved from using the web interface, the same can be said about moving to HTML. We are now only limited by what we can do with HTML, JavaScript and CSS.
- **Enhancement**: We can now utilize both custom and well-known CSS and JavaScript libraries to enhance our applications. Instead of making changes directly to the HTML or JavaScript, we can add entire libraries that can help us make further changes and enhancements to our dashboard.
- **Onboarding**: This is a major benefit of moving to HTML dashboards. Although Simple XML is not difficult to pick up, it is going to be a lot easier to have a new developer get up to speed if they are able to work with frameworks and libraries that they are already familiar with.

Making changes to HTML dashboards

Let's have a go at making some changes to our dashboard to show that it is straightforward; and all you need to do is just think about the setup of the code a little differently from what you did when it was set up in Simple XML. In this part of the chapter, we are going to change our chart to provide two separate line graphs for each for the companies that we are providing closing values for. This will mean that we will need to make changes to the HTML section, add another search manager for another search query, and then code a second visualization for the second line graph:

1. Log on to your development server, and as we have converted our Simple XML dashboard to HTML, the file for this dashboard will now be in the local directory of our Splunk App. So move to that directory:

```
cd $SPLUNK_HOME/etc/apps/stock_market/local/data/ui/html/
```

2. There should only be one file in the directory, so either use the Splunk Code Editor or use a text editor to open the `stock_market_historical_overview_html.html` file.

3. Move down to line 39 and change the heading element to now display a new heading relevant to the Splunk stock values. We can see this as follows:

```
39      <h3>Historical Overview of Splunk Closing Value</h3>
```

4. We move just past line 46 in our code where we have closed off the `div` container for `element1`. We are going to add the following lines to the code so that it will display a second graph:

```
47      <div id="row2" class="dashboard-row dashboard-row2">
48          <div id="panel1" class="dashboard-cell"
            style="width:100%;">
49              <div class="dashboard-panel clearfix">
```

5. We open up our `div` with `row2` as the ID for our second row, and we also name our second class `dashboard-row2`. We then set up the panel for the chart.

6. The following code can then be added where we set up the class for our new `panel-element`; name it `element2` and provide it with its own heading to reflect the data it is going to display:

```
51              <div class="panel-element-row">
52                  <div id="element2" class="dashboard-
                    element chart" style="width: 100%">
53                      <div class="panel-head">
54                          <h3>Historical Overview of Yahoo Closing
                            Value</h3>
55                      </div>
56                  <div class="panel-body"></div>
```

7. Now close off all of the `div` containers for this part of the HTML code:

```
57                      </div>
58                  </div>
59              </div>
60          </div>
61      </div>
```

8. We can now move down to the section of the code where our search managers are set up. We will first need to change the search query that is being run by the current search to only find and display the Splunk stock market data:

```
214          "search": "source="\*splkstock\.csv" | chart
             values(Close) AS Splunk by Date",
```

9. We now basically want to make a new search manager that will mirror the current one but specify Yahoo! as the subject of our search. We will add the following code lines after search1. With the additions that we have made so far, this should be at about line 223:

```
223          var search2 = new SearchManager({
224               "id": "search2",
225               "status_buckets": 0,
226               "earliest_time": "-1y@y",
227               "search": "source="\*yhoostock\.csv" | chart
                  values(Close) AS Yahoo by Date",
228               "latest_time": "$latest$",
229               "cancelOnUnload": true,
230               "app": utils.getCurrentApp(),
231               "auto_cancel": 90,
232               "preview": true,
233               "runWhenTimeIsUndefined": false
234          }, {tokens: true, tokenNamespace: "submitted"});
```

10. It is a simple addition where we call our new manager, search2, and our search will point to the Yahoo! stock market data. Each of the other options, including earliest and latest times, will be the same as search1.

11. We move down towards the bottom of the code where our visualization elements are set up. Currently, we have element1 already in place. If you remember, we have now entered a second element to be referenced within the HTML part of our code. As it will be very similar to element1, move just below this code and add the following code lines from line 281:

```
281          var element2 = new ChartElement({
282               "id": "element2",
283               "charting.chart": "bar",
284               "resizable": true,
285               "managerid": "search2",
286               "el": $('#element2')
287          }, {tokens: true, tokenNamespace: "
             submitted"}).render();
```

12. As you can see, we have set up the new visualization as `element2`, which simply references the new search manager we have now set up, called `search2`.

13. We save our changes, and we will also add this to our menu and navigation, as HTML dashboards are displayed a little bit differently. We move into our navigation directory for our Splunk App:

cd $SPLUNK_HOME/etc/apps/stock_market/default/data/ui/nav/

14. Open the `default.xml` file, and we will add an entry that will place the new dashboard on our interface and load it up when it is clicked. The following is the entire code for the `default.xml`, so you can see the difference between displaying Simple XML and HTML dashboards in our menu:

```
1 <nav search_view="search" color="#65A637">
2   <view name="overview" default='true' />
3   <a href="stock_market_historical_overview_html">Stock
    Market Historical Overview HTML</a>
4   <view name="search" />
5 </nav>
```

15. When we specify a Simple XML dashboard, we use the `view` element, but as you can see, we now use the anchor element with an `href` attribute to add our new HTML dashboard. We also need to specify the name that is going to be displayed in between the `tag` elements. If we do not specify the name to be displayed, it will display the filename and not the title as it did with our Simple XML dashboards.

16. Save your changes and reload the cache to your Splunk environment. If your changes have worked, you should be seeing something similar to the following screenshot:

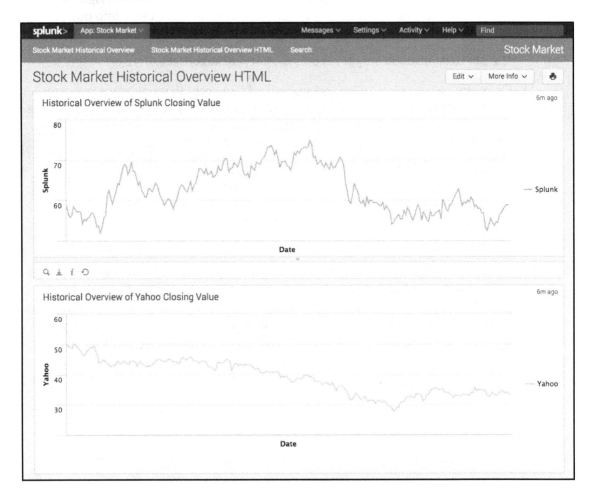

We now have our separate line charts displayed on the one dashboard and we have also been able to add a new item to the menu at the top of the screen.

 As you move further in this book, you will note that it may be getting harder to clear the cache in your Splunk environment. There may be some instances now when you are working with HTML and JavaScript where you will need to actually restart the Splunk daemon running on your environment.

So there seems to be a lot of code in the HTML section of our dashboard, but a lot of this code has been set up to improve the visual appeal of the information we are presenting to our users. The main reason why all of these visual elements are in place in our HTML is basically so that we can change and manipulate every tiny detail of the way our dashboard is displayed to our users. We are going to take this opportunity to quickly create a new dashboard that will remove all of the unnecessary code and only include the basic HTML code that we need to have our chart displayed on the page. Our new dashboard will be a copy of our original HTML dashboard so that we can compare the two:

1. If you are not already on your development server, log back in and move into the directory where your HTML dashboard is:

```
cd $SPLUNK_HOME/etc/apps/stock_market/local/data/ui/html/
```

2. Make a copy of the current dashboard; and we will create it with the word "raw" preceding the name:

```
cp stock_market_historical_overview_html.html
raw_stock_market_historical_overview_html.html
```

3. Open the new dashboard that you have now created with your text editor and remove the lines of code from line 18 to line 63 within the HTML section of the code.

4. We have now removed close to 50 lines of code, and all we are going to replace it with is the following line:

```
18 <p id="element1" />
```

5. Now we can also add this new HTML dashboard to our navigation, so move into the `nav` directory for our Splunk App:

```
cd $SPLUNK_HOME/etc/apps/stock_market/default/data/ui/nav/
```

6. Open the `default.xml` file with your text editor and add the following line after the previous HTML dashboard that we added:

```
4    <a href="raw_stock_market_historical_overview_html">Only
     A Graph Will be Displayed</a>
```

7. Save your changes and reload the cache for the Splunk environment. When you reload the stock market Splunk App, you will see that we have a new menu item named **Only A Graph Will be Displayed**. Select the menu item and you will now be presented with a very sparse dashboard page. It gives a good idea of how all the other items including the Splunk menus and headers are displayed.

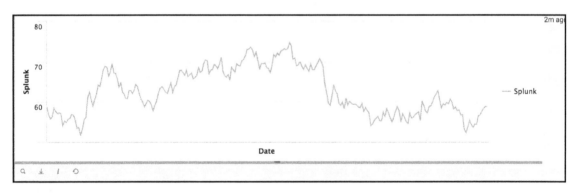

It may be rare that you actually want to display a dashboard in the way that we have done in the previous example. In my opinion, the exercise gives a really good example of where Splunk has such a great amount of power, and one of its major benefits lies in the way it is able to display data to your user.

In the following exercise, we are going to make a template from the Splunk App that we have just created. For me personally, I prefer to have all of my Splunk App code and configurations in the default directory of my Splunk App. I recommend that you copy the most recent HTML dashboards that we have created into a new `html` directory within the default directory of our Splunk App.

Creating a Splunk App template

We have created a three Splunk Apps so far, and in each of the instances, we used the barebones template from the Splunk web interface. We can, however, create our own template and add it to our Splunk environment to help streamline the process of creating our user interfaces.

In the example that we have been working on, we have been using stock market data to view different company stocks. What if we worked for a stock broking firm and wanted to create a separate Splunk App for each of our clients, or even better, create a separate Splunk App for each company stock values we were monitoring? Although our new example is not very extensive just yet, it could be, and if we were repeating work continuously, it would be a perfect reason to set up a template so that the process can be streamlined.

The Splunk App that you are creating your template from will need to be installed on the server that you are developing on, so log on to your development environment and you can perform some simple steps to get your template set up:

1. You may remember, Splunk comes with two templates currently available on your server, which are called barebones and `sample_app`. Move into the following directory and you will be able to see these templates firsthand:

   cd $SPLUNK_HOME/share/splunk/app_templates/

2. As long as our stock market Splunk App is set up the way that we want to as a template, you can simply copy the directory over to the `app_template` directory and this will set it up as a template for future use:

   cp -r $SPLUNK_HOME/etc/apps/stock_market $SPLUNK_HOME/share/splunk/app_templates/

3. You will need to restart your Splunk server for this change to take effect. Restart the server and log in to your environment. Use the web interface to create a new Splunk App like we have previously. If your changes have worked, you should see the `stock_market` template in our drop-down list of templates.

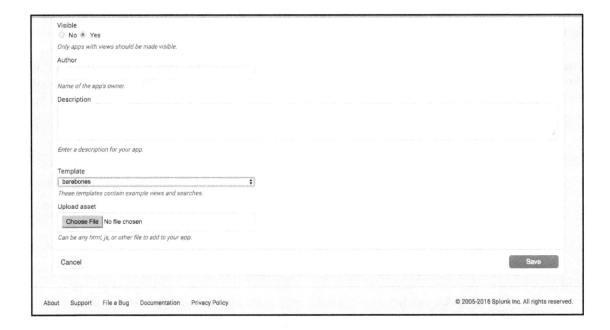

Summary

The work that we have been doing in this chapter is starting to get a little complex, so I hope you are still with us. In this chapter, we introduced our new example where we are starting to create our new Splunk App around stock market data provided by Yahoo! Finance. We created a basic Splunk App in Simple XML, but we then converted the main dashboard into an HTML dashboard using the Splunk web interface.

We went back in and explored how HTML is now displayed in the Splunk Code Editor. We then took a tour through the HTML code that we created, providing a run through and explanation of all the major parts of the code. We then had a further discussion on the benefits of moving to HTML dashboards and had a further look at how searches are coded in the HTML code. We finally implemented a template in our development environment to help fast-track our development process.

Our next chapter is going to look further into the JavaScript that we have created as part of converting the Simple XML dashboard into HTML. We will make some direct changes to the code to see what effect it has on our dashboard and we will start to work with native JavaScript libraries to add functionality to our Splunk App. We will also look at how we can create our own library or use a third-party library as part of our code.

7
JavaScript Modules in Your HTML App

You may have heard earlier that JavaScript is described as the language of the Internet. It is a widely used language and it is very rare these days that you access a website and not interact with JavaScript in some way. One of the main features of the Splunk Web Framework is the fact that it utilizes the power of JavaScript within its web interface. Although we have only spent one or two minor moments working with JavaScript, our dashboards have been using JavaScript since we created our first Splunk App.

In this chapter, we will continue to further develop our knowledge of the Splunk Web Framework, but we will focus more specifically on using and expanding JavaScript from within the HTML dashboard code. We will continue to expand our new Stock Market Splunk App and improve the visual appeal by working directly with the JavaScript code. In the chapter, we will cover the following topics:

- Learn where the JavaScript libraries in our Splunk installation are located and how they are used within our HTML code
- Make direct changes to the JavaScript in our dashboard to add extra functionality in the form of animation that responds to our user's mouse clicks
- Import and utilize native JavaScript libraries to add extra functionality to our dashboard
- Add third-party JavaScript libraries into our Splunk App to add extra functionality that may not be available by default within Splunk
- Finally, change the icons of our Splunk App to give it a little more individuality

JavaScript evolved out of a need to make web pages more dynamic and interactive. It was created by Netscape in 1995 with the main aim of the language to both be easy and allow non developers to understand, and also allow experienced developers greater control over what happened in the browser window. Since its creation it has become one of the essential building blocks of the web, found in most websites and supported by almost all web browsers.

In Splunk we can use JavaScript to help us control the visual appeal of the web interface, including structure and animation. In the next few pages, we will continue to work on our Stock Market Splunk App and add specific sets of functionality through JavaScript.

JavaSript modules in the Splunk Web Framework

Before we start working with some of the JavaScript modules, I thought it would be smart to point you in the direction of where the JavaScript modules are located in your Splunk installation. Some of the modules are not too advanced in terms of code that they utilize.

In the final chapter of this book, we will discuss in more depth what SplunkJS is and how to use it to get the most out of the Splunk Web Framework. SplunkJS is a set of components that will allow us to move our Splunk App away from using Splunk as a platform. For now though, we will continue to use the components as part of our dashboards as this is what the web interface uses to produce our dashboard and panel visualizations.

As we saw in our previous chapter, when we converted our Simple XML dashboard to HTML, the code is now specifically loading the modules that are in SplunkJS. The specific directory that is being used to contain these modules is as follows:

```
$SPLUNK_HOME/share/splunk/search_mrsparkle/exposed/js/splunkjs
```

From this directory, if you move into the `mvc` directory, things get a little clearer. In this directory, the JavaScript files are all named specifically with the functionality that they control:

- `headerview.js`: This specifies the way that headers of our dashboards and Splunk Apps are presented
- `chartview.js`: This specifically controls how the charts are presented to the end user

- `tableview.js`: When we provide a table of data instead of a chart, this is the JavaScript module that is used
- `textinput.js`: If we need to allow our users to interact with our forms, we can use this module to create a text input field

We could continue explaining all of the JavaScript modules in this directory, as there are times where you would need to work with each of them. It is useful to know that the modules are documented in the Splunk documentation and there are also comments through the code to explain what is occurring. Later in this chapter we will use some of these modules to expand the functionality of our dashboard, so you will get a first-hand example of how this is performed. If you want to find further information on the modules listed in SplunkJS and how to use them, refer to the Splunk component reference website `ht tp://docs.splunk.com/Documentation/WebFramework`.

Adding animation to Splunk dashboards

I use the term animation loosely as we are not going to be developing the next Pixar epic, but we will be working within our dashboard and enhancing the way that our dashboard panels work with the user's mouse clicks. We are going to continue working on the **Stock Market Historical Overview HTML** dashboard that we created in the previous chapter. We are currently displaying only two graphs on the page, but we will add JavaScript that will allow us to collapse the Yahoo! data so we can focus more on our Splunk stock market data. We will also add a table, but instead of just offering values, we add extra visual effects to allow it to switch between a row value and a graph.

If you have not done so already, you should move your HTML dashboard into the default directory of the Splunk App.

1. Log into your development server and move into the `html` directory where our dashboards are stored:

   cd $SPLUNK_HOME/etc/apps/stock_market/default/data/ui/html/

2. We want to make our dashboard place more focus on our Splunk stock market data. Open the `stock_market_historical_overview_html.html` file with your text editor and move down to line 28, where we are specifying the heading of the page, and change it to the following line:

   ```
   28 <h2>Stock Market Historical Overview Splunk</h2>
   ```

3. We are going to use a slide control to change the way the header of the second graph works. The graph will no longer be displayed on our page, only the heading will be available, so the user will know that there is some more information available, and hopefully this will be intuitive enough for the user to click and see more.

4. Move to the HTML code where we have specified our `div` containers to control the second graph for the Yahoo! stock market data. We are going to replace the code from line 51 with the following code:

```
51          <div class="panel-element-row">
52            <div class="panel-head"
              id="element2slideControl">
53                <h3>Comparison Overview of Yahoo
                  Closing Value - Click to Open/Close</h3>
54              </div>
55              <div id="element2" class="dashboard
                -element chart" style="width: 100%">
56                <div class="panel-body"></div>
57              </div>
58          </div>
```

5. In the preceding code, we have done a couple of things. The first thing we have done is that we have extended line 52 to now use the `slideControl` element that we are going to set up in the JavaScript section of the code. The second change is that we have changed the heading to show that the users can click on the heading to open and close the graph.

6. We now need to move down to the bottom of the file. We are using the `slideToggle` module to add this new feature to our dashboard. Fortunately, this is one of the default libraries loaded as part of the Splunk web application, specifically jQuery, so we do not need to load it into a variable like we have other libraries. We will be looking at importing libraries later in this chapter. For now, move down to the bottom of our file to a section of code under a comment called `DASHBOARD READY`. We need to add the next lines before this comment:

```
310          $("#element2slideControl").click(function(){
311            $("#element2").slideToggle("slow");
312            $("#panel2").resize();
313            element2.render();
314          }).click();
```

7. In the code, we are setting up the renderer for `element2`; specifically, we are going to create the `element2slideControl` that we added to our `div` container earlier. The previous code enables the `click` function of the `header` element to do the following:

- Slide at a slow speed, using the `slideToggle` library
- Enable the panel that we have set up as a graph to resize
- Click the heading when the page loads to ensure the graph is minimized as a default action

TIP

In the previous code, if you want your panel to be displayed in the open state when the page initially loads, you can simply leave off the `click()` function.

8. Save your changes, refresh the Splunk cache, and reload your page. Your dashboard will now be displayed with only the Splunk stock market values visible. However, when you click on the heading for the Yahoo! graph, it should open up and display as it did before we made the changes. Click on the heading again and it will collapse the graph, and look like the following screenshot:

I think that's a pretty cool change that we have made, ensuring that the page is more focused around the Splunk stock market data but still giving the option to allow a comparison with the Yahoo! data if that's what is needed. This now means that we have some more room available within our dashboard to provide some more information to our users. We are going to continue making changes to our JavaScript code, where we will add libraries to our code and make some changes to the way they work to enhance the functionality.

Ensuring your code is correct

Just before we move further into developing our code, I just want to give you a heads up that as the number of lines of code increases within our dashboards, there will be more chances for incorrect syntax to cause your pages to error or not load correctly. To give an example, the following section will require you to add new libraries into a statement in the JavaScript code. You will need to ensure that all the lines are separated with a comma (,) and if this does not occur, you will most likely be presented with a dashboard that will not load correctly and look similar to the following screenshot:

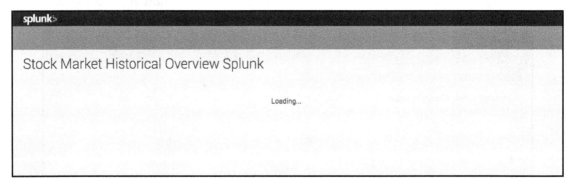

The dashboard is trying to load a library that cannot be found, and as a result will simply hang in the **Loading** state. I will try to do my best to point these issues out to minimize them from occurring, but as your experience grows, you will get used to the errors that you see. This is also where a good code editor will come in handy, as it will help point out potential issues for you.

Customizing JavaScript Modules in HTML

We are going to add a table to the bottom of the page to show the data for the highest open values for our stock market data. The table will be simple and only have two rows, but our changes to our JavaScript code will then allow the row to be expanded and display a timechart of the opening stock values.

1. You should still be in the html directory of your Splunk App. Open up the `stock_market_historical_overview_html.html` file in your text editor. We will start by adding in the div elements that will set up the table that will be displayed at the bottom of the page. Move down to line 62 of our code and add the following lines:

```
62    <div id="row3" class="dashboard-row dashboard-row3">
63        <div id="panel1" class="dashboard-cell"
          style="width: 100%;">
64            <div class="dashboard-panel clearfix">
65
66                <div class="panel-element-row">
67                    <div id="element3" class="dashboard
                      -element chart" style="width: 100%">
68                        <div class="panel-head">
69                            <h3>Stock Market Open Values -
                              Table with Expanding Rows</h3>
70
71                            <p>Click the > arrow on the
                              row to expand it!</p>
72                        </div>
73                        <div class="panel-body"></div>
74                    </div>
75                </div>
76            </div>
77        </div>
78    </div>
```

2. By now, you should be starting to get familiar with this type of change in your code. We are setting up a new row which will be labeled as `element3` and we have set up the heading to display **Open Values** for our stock market data. We have also added some extra information to guide our users to click on the > arrow on the table rows to display more information.

3. There are two libraries that we are going to load into our code and then make changes to them to add the functionality we need. Both these libraries are part of the Splunk installation, but we first need to add these libraries to the list of files that are required by this dashboard. If you move down to line 138 of the code, the list of libraries required is in alphabetical order, so the last library should be `splunkjs/mcv/simplexml/urltokenmodle`. JavaScript requires that a list of values needs to be separated by a comma. Make sure that you add a comma (,) at the end of the `urltokenmodel` entry and then add the next two lines of code:

```
138       "splunkjs/mvc/tableview",
139       "splunkjs/mvc/chartview"
```

4. Both these libraries are part of the `mvc` library, which we discussed earlier in this chapter, and are part of our Splunk installation. We don't load all the libraries available, as this will increase the time it takes for our page to load. Remember that both the libraries we have added can be viewed directly in the following location on your Splunk environment:

**$SPLUNK_HOME/share/splunk/search_mrsparkle/
exposed/js/splunkjs/mvc**

5. The libraries that we have just added need to be associated with a parameter name that is listed in the next part of the code. Move down to the end of this list, at line 175, and add the next two lines of code:

```
175          TableView,
176          ChartView
```

6. Make sure that you have added a comma (,) to the end of the previous line.

7. The `div` container that we set up for `element3` needs to have a search manager associated to it, to have the values populated through to the element. Move down the search manager section of the code and add the following lines of code to outline the way that the search manager will work and the specific search being run as part of the visualization:

```
257        var search3 = new SearchManager({
258            "id": "search3",
259            "status_buckets": 0,
260            "cancelOnUnload": true,
261            "latest_time": "$latest$",
262            "search": "sourcetype="stockcsv" | stats
               max(Open) AS HIGHEST_OPEN by source",
263            "earliest_time": "0",
264            "app": utils.getCurrentApp(),
265            "auto_cancel": 90,
266            "preview": true,
267            "runWhenTimeIsUndefined": false
268        }, {tokens: true, tokenNamespace: "submitted"});
```

8. Let's now set up the element section of the code where `element3` is defined and we specify how the visualization will be presented. The element ID is set up and we will be using the `TableView` library that we have just set up and loaded. The code also specifies the search that we have just set up:

```
324        var element3 = new TableView({ // Changed
           TableElement to TableView
325            "id": "element3",
326            "drilldown": "row",
327            "rowNumbers": "undefined",
328            "wrap": "undefined",
329            "managerid": "search3",
330            "el": $('#element3'),
331        }, {tokens: true, tokenNamespace:
           "submitted"}).render();
```

9. We have made a lot of changes to our page, and before we move onto the customization of the JavaScript code, we should make sure that the dashboard loads correctly before we make any more major changes.

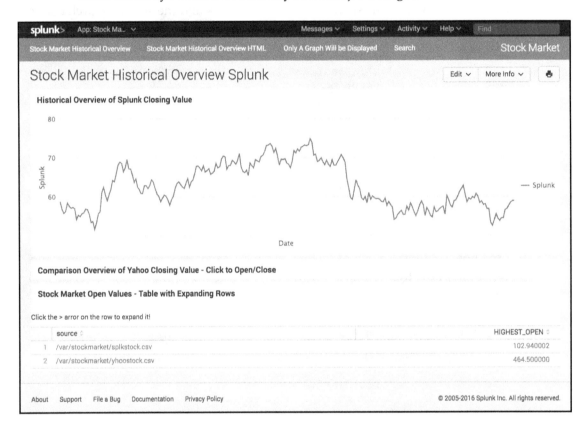

As we can see, the page is loading and the new table is available, but there are no arrows being displayed in each row. This is where we are now going to add this customization to our code.

To create the customization, we are going to need to create a JavaScript class that will extend the TableView library that we are importing as part of our page. Before we start to set up our code, let's walk through what we need to do with our customization. The new JavaScript code will need to do the following things:

- Create a new class that we are going to call it MyCustomRowRenderer, which will extend the BaseRowExpansionRenderer class, which is part of the TableView library

- Create an instance of our new class and use as part of the `element3` element that we have now set up as a table within our new dashboard

As part of this book, we haven't worked on something this complex as yet, so we might look at setting up the structure of the new class, and hopefully explain it a little better:

```
// Create the class and extend the BaseRowExpansionRenderer class
var CustomRowRenderer = TableView.BaseRowExpansionRenderer.extend({
initialize: function(args) {
  // Set up the new search manager to be used

  ...

  // Set up the new chart using chartView

  ...
  },

    // This is a required method as part of the framework
canRender: function(rowData) {

    ...
},

// Print the rowData object to the console and also return the value to be
parsed to the search manager and used in our query
render: function($container, rowData) {

...
});

  // Create the new search manager that will be used as part of our display
this._searchManager.set({

...
});

    // Display a graph rowData in the expanded row
    $container.append(this._chartView.render().el);
}

// And finally close off the class
});
```

Hopefully, walking through the class this way will make it easier to both explain and understand. There is still a lot of information that needs to be filled in before it is finished, but the general structure of the code will be as follows:

1. Create the class and extend the `BaseRowExpansionRenderer` class. This has been imported with the `TableView` library that we added into this dashboard file.
2. Set up the new search manager to be used, as we will need to generate a new search to fill the chart with data that we are going to create when the row is clicked.
3. Set up the new chart using the `chartView` class library that was imported to this dashboard code.
4. Set up the `canRender` module that is required as part of the framework code.
5. Then print the `rowData` object to the console. In this part of the code, we will return the value that will then be used and parsed to our search manager to be used in the search query.
6. Then use the `searchManager` class that we initialized. It will use the Splunk query as we normally would when searching data.
7. Finally, render our `chartView` object when the row value is clicked.

It seems pretty simple but we will step through the code and create the instance of the class to hopefully get your understanding straight. So log back into your development environment and we will get started with setting up this customization:

1. If you are not in the html directory of your Splunk App, do this now:

   cd $SPLUNK_HOME/etc/apps/stock_market/default/data/ui/html/

2. Open the `stock_market_historical_overview_html.html` file with your text or code editor.
3. Move down towards the bottom of our file and add the new class after line 348. We can start by adding our new class, which extends the `BaseRowExpansionRenderer` class, and we can start to initialize the new class:

```
348        // Create the class and extend the
           BaseRowExpansionRenderer class
349        var CustomRowRenderer =
           TableView.BaseRowExpansionRenderer.extend({
350            initialize: function(args) {
```

4. We set up our search manager as part of our initialization:

```
351              // Set up the new search manager to be
                 used
352              this._searchManager = new SearchManager({
353                  id: 'details-search-manager',
354                  preview: false
355              });
```

5. We then set up `chartView` as part of our initialization:

```
356              // Set up the new chart using chartView
357              this._chartView = new ChartView({
358                  managerid: 'details-search-manager',
359                  'charting.legend.placement': 'none'
360              });
361          },
```

6. We now set up the `canRender` function as part of the framework to render `rowData`:

```
363              // This is a required function as part of the
                 framework
364              canRender: function(rowData) {
365                  console.log("RowData: ", rowData);
366                  return true;
367              },
```

7. The next part of the class will set up `rowData` and help us define the information that we are going to use as part of our search. In our example, we have set up the table to provide the source value (Yahoo! or Splunk data). This will then be returned as a variable to be provided to our search query:

```
369              // Print the rowData object to the console
                 and also return the value to be parsed to the
                 search manager and used in our query
370              render: function($container, rowData) {
371              console.log("RowData: ", rowData);
372
373              var sourcetypeCell =
                 _(rowData.cells).find(function (cell) {
374                  return cell.field === 'source';
375              });
```

8. We can now use the `rowData` value returned and use it in a search manager. The query should look familiar to you by now:

```
377         // Create the new search manager that will be
            used as part of our display
378         this._searchManager.set({ search: 'source=' +
            sourcetypeCell.value + ' | chart values(Open) by
            Date'});
```

9. The class then displays the graph as a chart when the row is expanded. We also close off the class:

```
180         // Display a graph rowData in the expanded row
381         $container.append(this._chartView.render().el);
382             }
383         // And finally close off the class
384         });
```

10. We've done all the hard work and it's time to now use the class that we just created. We create an instance of the class called `myRowRenderer` and then we use that instance of the class and assign it to `element3` that we created earlier in the code:

```
386         var myRowRenderer = new CustomRowRenderer();
387         element3.addRowExpansionRenderer(myRowRenderer);
388         element3.render();
```

11. This is now the moment of truth. Save your changes and refresh the Splunk cache. If you have set up your JavaScript code correctly, you are about to see something pretty cool.

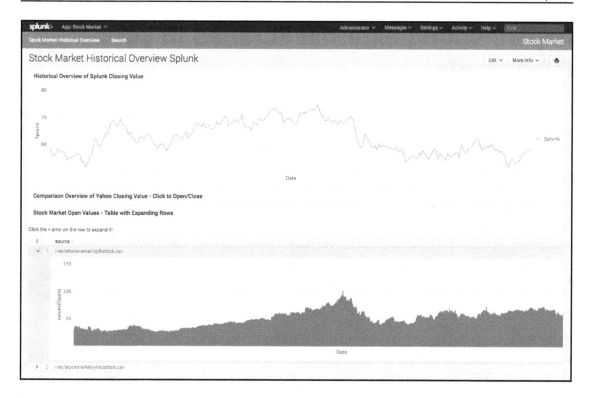

The first time I got this customization working I was pretty impressed, so I hope you are too. If the JavaScript class and the class instance is working correctly, you should now see arrows at the start of each row, and when you click on the arrow, it should expand down and produce a chart showing the opening stock market values by date. Although we have increased the amount of code in our `html` file by about 100 lines, we have added quite a number of animations and features for our users.

Implementing external libraries in your HTML code

Unless the library has been specifically designed as a Splunk library, implementing an external library into Splunk can be a very complex process with a large amount of coding to get through. For some of the more popular visualization libraries, such as D3 for example, there is extensive documentation on how to implement the specific library into a HTML web environment. The subject of implementing these types of libraries into the Splunk Web Framework could easily have its own book dedicated to it.

At the time of writing this book, there has been a lot of movement toward creating visualizations specifically for Splunk and the Splunkbase has a number of App installations available that extend the visualizations available to you on your environment. In this part of the book, we will use one of these freely available Splunk Apps to help streamline the process for us to implement an external library into our Stock Market Splunk App. At the same time, this will hopefully give you an indication of the work needed to perform this type of work on your own.

In the following pages, we are going to add the *D3 extensions for Splunk* Splunk App in our development environment, and we are going to implement the libraries used as part of this Splunk App in our example and configure it to work with the data that we have available. The specific Splunk App was created by Bernardo Macias and is available under the Apache License. It is freely available on the Splunkbase at `https://splunkbase.splunk.com/app/2856/#/overview`.

If you have not done so already, download and install this Splunk App onto your development environment. Load up the new Splunk App and you will see the following dashboard displayed by default:

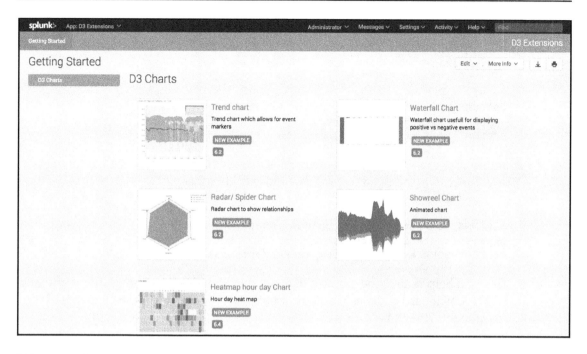

When you have it installed and you access the default dashboard, you will see that there are five different visualizations available. We are going to implement the heatmap visualization in our example. Feel free to look through the code before we move onto implementing the heatmap onto our dashboard.

Log back into your development environment and we will get started by implementing an external library into our Stock Market Splunk App:

1. We need to set up the directories that our JavaScript libraries will be located in, so move into the base of our Stock Market Splunk App:

   ```
   cd $SPLUNK_HOME/etc/apps/stock_market/
   ```

2. If you remember, in our previous chapters we have implemented JavaScript libraries into our Splunk App before, and as part of that we needed to make sure that the `appserver` and static directories have been created. Create these directories now:

   ```
   mkdir -p appserver/static
   ```

3. We want to copy the libraries from the *D3 extensions for Splunk,* and this can be done by copying the components directory from the D3 Splunk Extensions App into our example:

```
cp -r
$SPLUNK_HOME/etc/apps/d3_splunk_extentions/
appserver/static/components/*
$SPLUNK_HOME/etc/apps/stock_market/appserver/static/
```

4. Before we move on to using the libraries that we have set up in the components directories, we also need to copy one more file across:

```
cp
$SPLUNK_HOME/etc/apps/d3_splunk_extentions/
appserver/static/autodiscover.js
$SPLUNK_HOME/etc/apps/stock_market/appserver/static/
```

5. This will help reduce the amount of code that we will have to implement into our HTML dashboard code, as it will automatically instantiate all the elements in the components directory.

6. We can now start working on our HTML code to implement the external library. Move into the `html` directory of our Splunk App:

```
cd $SPLUNK_HOME/etc/apps/stock_market/default/data/ui/html/
```

7. Open the `stock_market_historical_overview_html.html` file with your text editor and we can start by setting up the div containers that will display our `heatmap` element. Move down to line 46 and start by adding a new panel in `row1`:

```
46          <div id="panel2" class="dashboard-cell"
            style="width: 50%;">
47              <div class="dashboard-panel clearfix">
48
49                  <div class="panel-element-row">
```

8. We have been adding new rows each time we have added a new panel to our dashboard. This time we are going to split the first row and add a second panel, resulting in our panel ID in line 46 being `panel2`.

9. As we continue, we will set up the new element as `element4` where we will set this code up in the JavaScript section of the code. The following code also includes the `h3` heading that we will use as part of our panel:

```
50      <div id="element4" class="dashboard-element
        chart" style="width: 100%">
51          <div class="panel-head">
52              <h3>Closing Stock Value
                Heatmap</h3>
53          </div>
54      <div class="panel-body"></div>
```

10. The next part of the code will set our heatmap visualization, including the location of the library being used in the components directory that we have just set up. It also allows us to configure the search that will be used as part of the visualization, the height and width, and finally we will be using the `valueField` of the Close stock market value to be displayed:

```
55      <div id="heatmaphourday" class="splunk-view"
        data-require="app/stock_market/
        components/heatmap_dayhou    r/heatmap_dayhour"
        data-options='{"managerid":"search4",
        "height":"400","width":"100","valueField":"Close"}
        '></div>
```

11. In line 55, the data-require and data-options attributes are also needed as they not only ensure that the visualization is located but are required for auto discovery to work correctly.

12. The rest of the HTML-specific code will close off the `div` elements:

```
56                      </div>
57                  </div>
58              </div>
59      </div>
```

13. Move down to the search manager section of the code and we will set up the search that we are going to use as part of the display. The search is a lot more involved than what we have previously used as it turns our date value into a `unix` timestamp so we can extract the day of the week value:

```
284     var search4 = new SearchManager({
285         "id": "search4",
286         "search": "source="\*splkstock\.csv"
            | eval date_epoch = strptime('Date', "%Y-%m-%d")
            | eval day=strftime(date_epoch, "%w")
```

```
                    | stats values(day) As day, values(Day) AS time
                  by Close",
287                   "earliest_time": "$earliest$",
288                   "sample_ratio": null,
289                   "status_buckets": 0,
290                   "latest_time": "$latest$",
291                   "cancelOnUnload": true,
292                   "app": utils.getCurrentApp(),
293                   "auto_cancel": 90,
294                   "preview": true,
295                   "runWhenTimeIsUndefined": false
296               }, {tokens: true, tokenNamespace: "submitted"});
```

We have cheated a little here. The stock market data does not give us an hour of day value. In our example, we are simulating this by using the day of the month value as the time value. We are still able to get a good grasp of where the larger close values are being represented in our data, but the example is more focused directly on how to implement the JavaScript library into our Splunk App.

14. We now need to move down towards the end of the code, just after where we specified our element3 renderer that we set up in the previous part of this chapter. We can now add the following code to render the element4 code:

```
417 var element4 = new HtmlElement({
418 "id": "element4",
419 "useTokens": true,
420 "el": $('#element4')
421 }, {tokens: true, tokenNamespace:
    " submitted"}).render();
```

15. Finally, we need to load in all the libraries that we will be using as part of our code. Instead of adding them to our require statement, like we have in the previous examples, we simply need to load the autodiscover.js file that we discussed earlier:

```
433 <script src="
    {{SPLUNKWEB_URL_PREFIX}}/static/app/stock_market/
    autodiscover.js" type="text/javascript"></script>
```

16. Save your code and reload the Splunk cache to make the new code active in your Splunk App. Load the page and you should now see something similar to the following image:

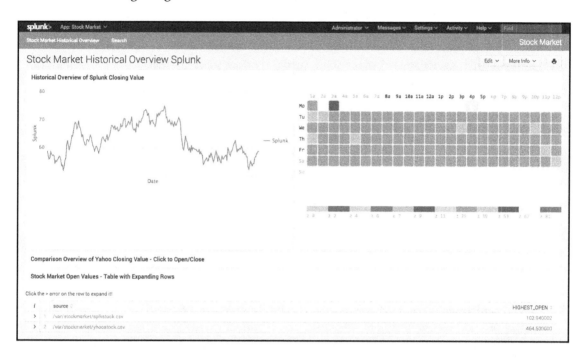

This is a great example of external JavaScript libraries that we can use to extend what Splunk officially provides in the default installation. If you are interested in the specific code for the heatmap visualization, move into the following directory that we set up earlier:

```
cd $SPLUNK_HOME/etc/apps/stock_market/appserver/
static/components/hearmap_dayhour
```

If you open the `heatmap_dayhour.js` file, it is just under 200 lines of code, which does not seem too involved, but note that it relies on four or five other libraries, including the D3 set of libraries, and Splunk view and `mvc` libraries. There is a lot of inter-related code that need to be taken into consideration before your visualization will work as desired.

Adding your icon to your Splunk App

So far in this chapter, we have been using the `appserer` and static directories to add JavaScript libraries to our Splunk App to help add extra functionality to our users. Just before we finish up this chapter, I thought it would be a good time to show you where you can also add icon images to your Splunk App and the Splunk Web Framework will automatically pick them up and place them into the home page listing, the Splunk search bar and your App Bar of your Splunk App.

There are lots of free icons available for use. We have selected the following icon for our Stock Market Splunk App, which I think sums up what we are trying to achieve:

The preceding icon is made by Freepik and can be downloaded from `http://www.flaticon.com/`, and we will be using this to add it into our environment. The Splunk Web Framework will place our icon into specific parts of our Splunk App based on the name that we assign to it:

- `appIcon.png`: This will place the icon on the Splunk home page under our specific Splunk App in standard resolution
- `appIcon_2x.png`: This will place the icon on the Splunk home page under our specific Splunk App in high resolution
- `appIconAlt.png`: This will place the icon on the App menus for the Splunk bar and search bar in standard resolution
- `appIconAlt_2x.png`: This will place the icon on the App menus for the Splunk bar and search bar in high resolution
- `appLogo.png`: This will place the icon on the App bar that is in the top right-hand corner of our Splunk App in standard resolution
- `appLogo_2x.png`: This will place the icon on the App bar that is in the top right-hand corner of our Splunk App in high resolution

In our example, we are going to add the icon to the Splunk home page and the search bar. We won't add it to our App bar as it will replace the Stock Market text that we currently have in place, and I think this text gives a good explanation of what the Splunk App does. Log back into your development environment and we will show you the changes you can make to add your logo to your Splunk App:

1. We will start by changing to the base of our Stock Market Splunk App:

   ```
   cd $SPLUNK_HOME/etc/apps/stock_market/
   ```

2. We already have a static directory in the appserver directory where we have been setting up a lot of our JavaScript libraries. When it comes to icons, we now need to make a new static directory in the base of our Splunk App as well:

   ```
   mkdir $SPLUNK_HOME/etc/apps/stock_market/static
   ```

3. The previous icon can be downloaded from this chapters resource download, or you can download your own if you have a better icon idea or image. We want to place this icon in the new static directory that we have created.

4. Make a copy of the icon, rename the image appIcon_2x.png, and place it in the new static directory we created:

   ```
   cp appIcon_2x.png $SPLUNK_HOME/etc/apps/stock_market/static
   ```

5. This file will be used as part of the Splunk home page.

6. We want to do the same thing again, but this time we want to name it appIconAlt_2x.png and place it in our static directory as well:

   ```
   cp appIconAlt_2x.png
   $SPLUNK_HOME/etc/apps/stock_market/static
   ```

7. This file will be used as part of the **App** menu.

8. That's about all there is to it. Refresh the Splunk cache and then reload the home page of our development environment.

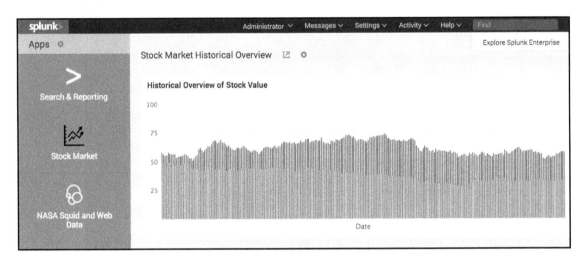

After the minor changes we just made, we can see that our Stock Market Splunk App now has a shiny new icon associated with it in the welcome page. We can also see in the following image that when we use the app menu, our Stock Market Splunk App also has our icon associated with it:

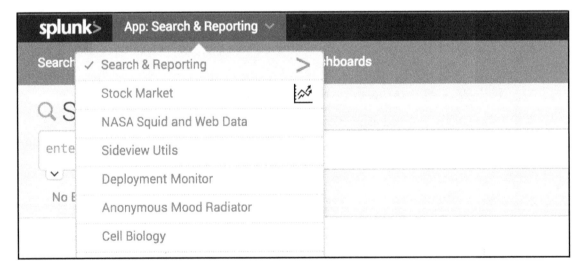

I hope you are happy with what we have achieved in this chapter and it's time to start wrapping things up so we can move onto our next subject.

Summary

Our Stock Market Splunk App is starting to look attractive and the work we are doing with this example is starting to get into the more advanced areas of the Splunk Web Framework. In this chapter, we looked through the JavaScript in our HTML code and discussed where we can find the different JavaScript libraries that are installed by default in our environment. We made direct changes to the JavaScript section of our code to add extra functionality, as well as made direct changes to extend the functionality of some of the native JavaScript libraries.

We also looked at third-party JavaScript libraries and we added a D3 visualization to our example to give it some more visual appeal. In the final part of this chapter, we saw how easy it is to change the Splunk App icons being displayed to our users.

In our next chapter, we are going to move from JavaScript to CSS and explore the CSS format of the HTML code layout, and how to make use of the inline CSS section to make changes to our Splunk App. We will look at overriding the default Splunk Color schemes and styles to give our dashboards extra individuality and visual appeal.

8
Utilizing CSS to Spice Up Visual Appeal

My original experience with CSS was a very short journey through the basics of what CSS does and can do. I actually didn't see the point in all of it though. I saw the basic elements and structure of HTML to be just fine for what I was doing and and felt no need to worry about CSS. As the years went on though, I saw that most companies like to control the look, layout, and color scheme of their sites to the tiniest degree, with no exception on the font and color scheme that they specifically felt characterizes their company values.

Although I'm not a designer, I needed to start being aware of how to manipulate the format and structure of dashboards and pages that I was creating, and the more I learned about the things you can do with CSS the more I wanted to use it.

We are going to look at customizing the style of our Splunk App to suit our needs and share some ideas on how to improve the visual appeal of our Splunk App. We are also going to move away a little from the default Splunk color scheme and display. In this chapter, we will do the following:

- Discuss CSS templates and themes, and how they can be used within your Splunk App dashboard
- Look at the different ways that CSS can be used within our HTML code and implement examples into our Stock Market Splunk App
- Work with standard CSS libraries that are available to us within our Splunk installation to make changes to our dashboards
- Look at some external CSS libraries and how we can utilize their functionalities to change the way our dashboard looks

CSS stands for **Cascading Style Sheets** and describes how HTML elements are to be displayed in your application. CSS can save you a lot of work as it can control the layout of multiple web pages all at once, as we can store style sheets externally as CSS files. With external styles sheet files we can change the look of an entire website by changing just one file.

I think we have a great place to start working with CSS. Earlier in this book, as part of our Stock Market Splunk App, we created a *raw* version of our historical overview of our data to demonstrate the most minimalistic version of our HTML dashboard. We can use this dashboard to implement imported themes as well as create our own CSS to suit our own requirements, which may be needed if setting up a Splunk App or dashboard that is to adhere to specific company standards or schemes.

CSS templates and themes

Customizing your Splunk App is simple when using CSS, but you need to be careful when using a template, as your overriding specific Splunk Themes could result in your dashboard looking and operating in a manner that may firstly be unattractive to your users and secondly may render specific functionality useless.

For now, we are going to use our raw dashboard as there is not much added in the way of functionality that an external template or theme will cause any problems for. Searching on the Internet will give you endless options in the way of CSS themes and templates that have already been created for you to download free of change and implement into your own websites. The company you are working for may also have their own CSS Theme that needs to be used within your Splunk App.

In the following pages, we are going to make use of a free CSS theme that we will download from `http://bootswatch.com/`, specifically a theme called **United**. Let's get started with this simple change. Log back into your development environment and follow these next steps:

1. We have worked with the static directory previously. This is where we need to start to make these changes, so move into this directory:

   `cd $SPLUNK_HOME/etc/apps/stock_market/appserver/static/`

2. We are going to download the bootstrap.min.css file from the following URL: `htt ps://bootswatch.com/united/`.

3. We now need to let our dashboard know that it needs to use this new theme. Move back to our `html` directory, and we can add this external CSS file to our raw dashboard:

```
cd $SPLUNK_HOME/etc/apps/stock_market/default/data/ui/html/
```

4. Open the `raw_stock_market_historical_overview_html.html` file with your code or text editor. We are going to make a minor change to our code.

5. In the head of our HTML code, move just below the default CSS files that Splunk uses to set up our dashboard code, and add the following line:

```
10              <link rel="stylesheet" type="text/css" href="
                {{SPLUNKWEB_URL_PREFIX}}/static/app/stock_market/
                bootstrap.min.css" />
```

6. All we are doing here is asking for the new United CSS theme to be loaded into our HTML page.

7. Save your changes and refresh your Splunk cache to let these changes take effect.

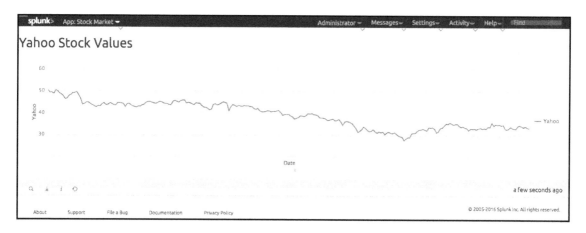

You would have seen the theme on the Bootswatch website and it looks pretty cool. For our dashboard, so far there is not too much involved so adding our new theme only adds some minor changes to our raw dashboard compared to what it was previously. I think this theme will look pretty cool when we start to add more elements to the page. So we will continue to work with this theme for the remainder of this chapter but we will add in a number of customizations in line with this theme to make it our own.

When you select one of the other dashboards in our Stock Market Splunk App, you will note that the theme of the dashboard is back to the original Splunk theme, as we have only added this theme to our raw dashboard.

> When you use Splunk, you still need to make sure that you give credit for the work that the developers at Splunk have been doing. Make sure that you include the Splunk or Splunk Powered logos within your apps to ensure that you give the correct credit when it's due. We will be correcting this shortly with our raw dashboard, and if you need more information on Splunk branding policies, consult the Splunk website.

Get the raw dashboard ready

We need to get our `raw_stock_market_historical_overview_html` into a state that we can start to work with our CSS code. To get the dashboard ready, we are going to change our dashboard to be specific for the Yahoo! stock market data values. We are going to add the Splunk header and footer in our dashboard and make sure people know that the dashboard and data is being created by Splunk. We will also add a heading. We are still going to keep this dashboard in a minimalist state, so we can work with CSS and make enhancements with that part of the code.

Even though we won't directly be working with CSS in the following few pages, it will enforce some of the work that we did in the previous two chapters. Get back into our development environment and let's start to get our dashboard looking a little less raw:

1. We will go directly into making changes to our raw dashboard, so move into the `html` directory of our Stock Market Splunk App:

    cd $SPLUNK_HOME/etc/apps/stock_market/default/data/ui/html/

2. Open the `raw_stock_market_historical_overview_html`.html file with your text or code editor.

3. As we said a little earlier, we should be adding the Splunk header back into our Splunk App, so that the users know we are using Splunk to create the data and using it as a platform for our App. Move down to line 19 and add in the following line:

    ```
    19 <div class="header splunk-header"></div>
    ```

4. Leave one or two lines, and then add in a heading element to show that this dashboard will be displaying Yahoo! stock market data:

```
21 <h2>Yahoo Stock Values</h2>
```

5. We can now move down past element1 that runs our graph and add in the Splunk footer:

```
25 <div class="footer splunk-footer"></div>
```

6. Move down to where we define what the element will be displaying, and we are currently displaying search1 for element1. This will give us more Splunk stock market data though, so we need to change this. The easiest way to do this is by changing which search element1 is pointing to. Move down to the block of code that specifies element1 and change it to the following:

```
234         var element1 = new ChartElement({
235             "id": "element1",
236             "charting.chart": "line",
237             "resizable": true,
238             "managerid": "search2",
239             "el": $('#element1')
240         }, {tokens: true, tokenNamespace:
            "submitted"}).render();
```

7. Line 238 now specifies search2 as the managerid. We originally set this up in our previous chapter to search for Yahoo! stock market data, so we may as well use it.

8. Finally, we want to make a change to the way our Splunk header displays. We added this in step 3 of the work we have been performing. This change will add both the Splunk application bar as well as our **Stock Market Splunk App** menu items into the header. We are going to define our own **App** menu in CSS shortly, so we can remove this from the header. Move to where the header items are specified, which is around line 200:

```
201         new HeaderView({
202             id: 'header',
203             section: 'dashboards',
204             el: $('.header'),
205             acceleratedAppNav: true,
206             useSessionStorageCache: true,
207             splunkbar: true,
208             appbar: false,
209             litebar: false,
210         }, {tokens: true}).render();
```

9. As you can see in line 208, the value of appbar is now false, which will give us the desired results.

10. Save your changes and refresh the Splunk cache. We should now see that our raw dashboard, while still looking pretty raw, at least has a header, footer, and a heading. All of these are now themed with the United template that we added at the start of this chapter. The Splunk header and footer still work as they should.

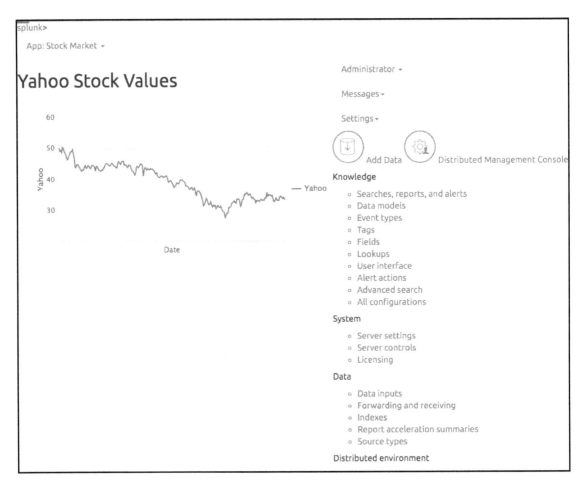

Although we have continued to use some of the in-built Splunk CSS, it has been affected by the new theme we have added. If you click on the **Settings** option in the Splunk menu at the top right of the dashboard, you will note that all the fonts have been changed to the same color as the **United Theme**.

Our dashboard still uses quite a few Splunk CSS features though and we need to make sure that we are still utilizing the original Splunk `bootstrap.min.css` that comes with our installation of Splunk. As we mentioned earlier in this chapter, adding themes to our Splunk App could cause a lot of problems if we are not careful. For example, if we were to remove or comment out line 8 on the raw dashboard, it would cause a lot of problems with our Splunk header, footer, and visualizations:

```
8 <!--          <link rel="stylesheet" type="text/css" href="/en-
US/static/@264376/css/build/bootstrap.min.css" /> -->
```

It may be hard to give you the full visual impact of the change, but the following image shows what happens when the changes are saved and the Splunk cache is reloaded. Our visualization is on the page but it is all scrunched up because the Splunk menu is spread across the rest of our page. If you have made this change as a test, change it back before moving forward with this chapter.

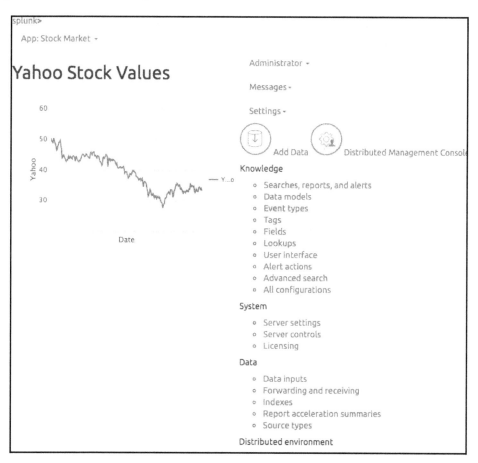

As you can see in the preceding image, we have virtually rendered the dashboard useless by removing our main Splunk CSS. Fortunately, in this example we only have one visualization on the page, but if we had more, it would most likely be cutting off a majority of the data, both confusing our users and putting them off from using the dashboard.

Implementing your own CSS style

We can now start to implement CSS in our dashboard code to change the look and appearance of our visualizations, headings, text, and background colors, to name only a few. As with most CSS implemented in HTML code, within a Splunk HTML dashboard, there are three ways that we can incorporate CSS:

- **Inline style**: We can specify the styles of the specific element directly when we announce it in the code.
- **Internal style sheet**: This is where we can define the style sheet rules within the header of our HTML code using the style element.
- **External style sheet**: We can also define rules in a separate .css file within our Splunkenvironment and then refer back to this set of style sheet from within our dashboard HTML code. An external style sheet is the preferred method to define your style as there is less chance of having to duplicate your code across a project.

If you have not worked with CSS before, you specify a set of rules for a specific group of elements by specifying a selector and then implement a declaration:

- **Selector**: This is the actual element that you would be defining. For the next example, we use the h1 heading element and this would be set up as h1 in our CSS rule. You will see later in this chapter that to make sure specific style definitions are not confused, we can also specify an alternative name as a class name.
- **Declaration**: The declaration is usually a set of properties and values that then control the way the selector will look. For example, we can set the size as the property and the number of pixels as the value.

In our code, we would have the rule set up as follows:

```
h1 {
color:green;
margin-left:30px;
font-size:24px;
}
```

The preceding example specifies the h1 element to be green in color, extend from the left margin by thirty pixels, and have the font size as twenty-four pixels in size. As you can see, we have specified this rule across a number of lines to make it easier to read, but you can also perform this definition in one line as we will see in the next part of the chapter.

Inline style sheets

We can specify the style of the element that we are working on whenever we want to change the way that a specific element is to look. Using CSS in this way is not very efficient and will only change the styles of the specific element we are working on. For example, if we want all the h1 heading elements in our dashboard to use a specific color, we need to make this same change every time we use the h1 element. It would be a lot easier to set up the CSS as part of the header or as part of an external CSS file, so we can use it for all our HTML code.

Defining styles inline would only be used for one off corrections or changes, and it would be very limited in the instances that you would be using this type of rule definition. In our example, we will make a quick change to the way our heading is currently displayed to give you an idea of how the Splunk HTML code will use an inline style definition. Log back into your development environment and we will get started:

1. Move into the html directory of our Stock Market Splunk App, so we can make the change to our heading that we have just set up:

   ```
   cd $SPLUNK_HOME/etc/apps/stock_market/default/data/ui/html/
   ```

2. Move down to line 21 of our HTML code and you will see that we have set out our h2 element for the Yahoo Stock Values heading. We are going to make a minor change to specify some style, and change it to the following line:

   ```
   21 <h2 style="color:blue;margin-left:30px;">Yahoo Stock
      Values</h2>
   ```

3. In our example, we have set the color as blue, but we could also specify it as a three value hexadecimal value. We have also set the distance of the heading from the left margin at 30 pixels. As you can see, we use the style attribute to declare the rules for this h2 element. Text color in blue usually implies an unvisited link, so this example is not something that you would want to implement unless you had this text linked to adhere to web standards.

4. Save the code changes that you have made and refresh the Splunk cache in your development environment. Reload the raw dashboard and you should now see that we have a heading for our dashboard that is a lot clearer to read when compared against the new United theme that we implemented.

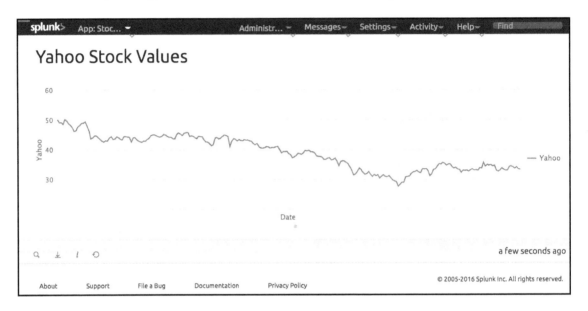

Not much of a change, but it's still useful to know. There are few times that you would use this type of CSS definition, so we will try to limit the times that we use this type of style definition. We will continue to work with our raw Splunk dashboard but move onto more efficient ways of working with CSS.

Using internal style sheets in your Splunkcode

As we discussed earlier in this chapter, another way in which you can use CSS is by specifying the style as part of your header within the `html` code itself. This also is not the most efficient way of using CSS as it means that you would need to add the style block to all the pages that you would like to look the same.

Personally, I like to use internal style sheets to establish a set of styles that I am happy with and would like to implement across a number of pages. Once I can verify that I have all my styles working as they should be, I then move these rules into an external CSS file. This is what we are going to do with our example to show you how Splunk Web Framework allows you to define both internal and external style sheets within your Splunk dashboards. In the next part of this chapter, we will set up internal style rules where we will set up a menu for the dashboard that will sit on the right side of our dashboard screen. We will then use these style definitions as the base of our external style sheet to be used with our raw dashboard.

CSS and dashboard menus

We have been using the Splunk Web Framework to set up our menus for quite a few chapters now. Splunkmenus are limited in the way we can control the look and feel of how the menu works and there is not much in the way of individualization or customization. If you have worked with CSS before, you would be familiar with setting up menus across the top or side of your HTML documents. We are going to quickly add some CSS to the header of our raw dashboard to set up a menu on the side of our screen. Let's start working through the code and we will step through the CSS and changes you need to make to get this working, as we have in the previous chapters:

1. We should still be in our development environment and working in our html directory, but if not, move into the html directory of our Stock Market Splunk App:

   ```
   cd $SPLUNK_HOME/etc/apps/stock_market/default/data/ui/html/
   ```

2. Open up the `raw_stock_market_historical_overview_html.html` file in your text or code editor, so we can add CSS to our dashboard code. Back in Chapter 6, *Moving from Simple XML to HTML*, when we looked through the code of our converted HTML dashboard, we discussed the header of our HTML code, and within the first 10 lines of the code, we have our CSS styles sheets being referenced within these lines. We are going to add in our own style definitions just below these lines of code.

    As we mentioned in our previous chapter, mixing CSS from different sources can cause our page to have issues with specificity and in turn not allow our dashboard to display the way we want. We are mixing style definition types in our page as an example of how to get started and this should be planned carefully at an earlier stage of development.

3. Move down to line 12 and we will kick off our style definitions for our menu with the style element. We will set the margin of the body of the dashboard to zero:

```
12 <style>
13 body {
14 margin: 0;
15 }
```

4. Our menu is basically going to be an unordered list and a set of list elements, but by specifying the way they act, we can have it look like a nice menu on the side of our screen. So we don't mess up an other CSS that might already be set up and we could be using within our header or chart elements, we will set up our styles with a class name of side:

```
17 ul.side {
18     list-style-type: none;
19     margin: 0;
20     padding: 0;
21     width: 25%;
22     position: fixed;
23     overflow: auto;
24     background-color: #e6f2ff;
25 }
```

5. The code that we just added is nothing too complex. We are simply defining margins, width, padding, and position, among other things. All of these will be used by the elements when we work with them in the body section of our dashboard code.

6. We can now specify the definitions of the list elements and how they work within our dashboard:

```
26 li.side a {
27     display: block;
28     color: #000;
29     padding: 8px 0 8px 16px;
30     color: red;
31 }
```

7. The preceding definitions specify how the menu items will act when there are no specific actions occurring.

8. The next part of the style rule defines how the list item menus will act when we hover over the items, and how they will act when they are active:

```
34 li.side a.active {
35     background-color: #4CAF50;
36     color: white;
37 }
38
39 li.side a:hover:not(.active) {
40     /* This will not be compatible with IE8 or earlier
41     background-color: #555;
42     color: white;
43 }
44 </style>
```

9. Don't forget line 43, where we close off the style element on our header code.

10. Now move down to the body section of our dashboard code and we can use the new element classes that we have just defined. Within the body of the dashboard code, move just past the div container we have specified to use the Splunk header code and add the following unordered list:

```
55 <ul class="side">
56     <li class="side"><a href="overview">Overview</a></li>
57     <li class="side"><a
       href="stock_market_historical_overview_html">Splunk
       Historical Overview</a></li>
58     <li class="side"><a class="active"
       href="newraw_stock_market_historical_overview_html">
       Yahoo Historical Overview</a></li>
59     <li class="side"><a href="search">Search</a></li>
60 </ul>
```

11. As you can see, we are using the specific class that we created, called side, for both the unordered list (ul) and list (li) elements. For each of the list elements, we have simply referenced each of the dashboards that we have created within our Splunk App so far. You will note that the overview and search Simple XML dashboards are simply referenced with the basic filename with no extensions. However, we do need to specify the entire file name for the html dashboards, and in this instance we have provided names that are a little more descriptive of the information they are displaying.

12. To make sure that our menu and our graph is properly separated, we will enclose our visualization and heading in a div element. Move down to where we specified the original heading and graph elements and replace them with the following lines of code:

```
62 <div style="margin-left:25%;padding:1px
   16px;height:1000px;">
63     <h2 style="color:blue;margin-left:30px;">Yahoo Stock
       Values</h2>
64     <p id="element1" />
65 </div>
```

13. Save your code and reload your Splunk cache. You should now have a menu added to the left side of your dashboard:

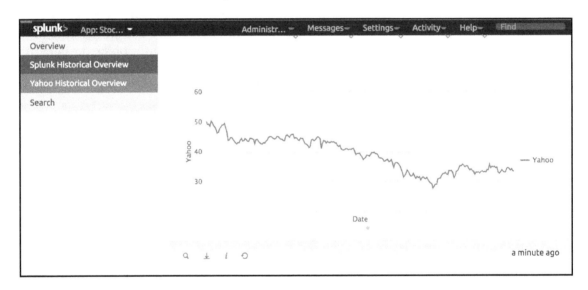

Hopefully, your dashboard looks the same as the preceding image, where we have a nicely styled menu sitting on the side of our page which links directly to the other pages in our Stock Market Splunk App. The current dashboard that is available will be highlighted in green, and when our mouse pointer hovers over one of the other menu items, as in the preceding image, it will be highlighted in dark grey. We have also made the names of our Splunk and Yahoo! stock market data dashboards a little more descriptive.

CSS is not really that difficult to master. It is there for us to add consistency in our dashboards and Splunk Apps. By doing a little bit of hard work and planning at the start of your project, it will save you a lot more time in the long run.

Setting up external style sheets in Splunkapps

When it comes to CSS, external style sheets are the implementation type that you would want to be aiming for when developing with HTML dashboards. An external style sheet will be made available in one central location and reusable across all your code within your environment, and if hosted on a web server, would be available across multiple environments and locations.

In our previous example, we set up some internal style definitions to set up how our menu will look and operate, and it seems like the perfect opportunity to move these style definitions into an external CSS file. Log back into your development environment and we will get started with setting up an external style sheet to be used in our dashboard code:

1. We have been working with our static files and directories recently, and this is where we are going to set up our external CSS file. So move into our static directory at the following location:

   cd $SPLUNK_HOME/etc/apps/stock_market/appserver/static/

2. Create a new file with your code or text editor and call it stock_market_rules.css.

3. We can now transfer the rules that we created to set up our menu for our raw dashboard. We can start by adding in the body element and the unordered list that is set up under the side class name:

```
 1 body {
 2     margin: 0;
 3 }
 4
 5 ul.side {
 6     list-style-type: none;
 7     margin: 0;
 8     padding: 0;
 9     width: 25%;
10     position: fixed;
11     overflow: auto;
12     background-color: #e6f2ff;
13 }
```

4. Now enter the remaining lines of our side class style definition that refer to the list elements:

```
14 li.side a {
15     display: block;
16     color: #000;
17     padding: 8px 0 8px 16px;
18     text-decoration: none;
19     color: red;
20 }
21
22 li.side a.active {
23     background-color: #4CAF50;
24     color: white;
25 }
26
27 li.side a:hover:not(.active) {
28     background-color: #555;
29     color: white;
30 }
```

5. Save this file.

6. Now open the `raw_stock_market_historical_overview_html.html` file again. We now need to add a reference to the new external CSS file that we have just created. We will add this to the header of the HTML. You may remember that at the start of this chapter we added our first external CSS file that set up the **United** theme for our dashboard. We will add our new external CSS file just below that by adding in the following line of code:

```
12          <link rel="stylesheet" type="text/css" href="
            {{SPLUNKWEB_URL_PREFIX}}/static/app/stock_market/
            stock_market_rules.css" />
```

7. Make note of the location that we are using when specifying the external CSS file as it is not the exact directory location of the file, but is understandable by our Splunk installation.

8. We no longer have a need for the internal style definitions that we set up previously, so all we need to do now is delete all the internal style definitions. This should be all the code in between the style opening and closing tags, from approximately line 13 to 55.

9. Once again, save your changes and reload your Splunk cache. You should not see any further change as the CSS that we previously loaded internally is now being loaded from our external CSS file.

Using the Splunk Web Framework CSS

So far in this chapter, we have imported an external CSS Theme and have been working on our own external CSS file to create and manipulate the style rules of our HTML code. A lot of the work is already done for us though, as Splunk comes with CSS built into the web framework to allow web developers with knowledge of well-known frameworks to start building within the Splunk Web Framework easily and quickly.

One of the most well known of these frameworks is Bootstrap and as we have discussed previously, it comes with our Splunk environment installation. Bootstrap is a free frontend framework that allows fast and easy web development and includes HTML and CSS-based design templates for a large range of elements, including buttons, tables, forms, navigation, fonts, images, and many more. It also includes JavaScript plugins to provide further functionality.

In the next part of this chapter, we will continue to work with our raw dashboard and utilize some of the features that Bootstrap provides us. Hopefully you will see that it is easy to use, has a load of features, and is compatible with most modern web browsers. By using a framework that has already been established, you will see that it allows us to implement these features more rapidly than sorting our code by ourselves.

In our work, we have been linking our dashboard HTML code to the version of Bootstrap that we have installed as part of our Splunk installation. If we wanted the most up-to-date version, we could download it directly and install it into our static directory, as we have been doing so far with our external CSS files. The latest version can be downloaded from `http://getbootstrap.com`.

Instead of having to download this file and update every time there is a change, we can point to the content delivery network for Bootstrap, which would be similar to the following URL: `http://maxcdn.bootstrapcdn.com/bootstrap/3.3.6/css/bootstrap.min.css`.

For a full list of features and documentation on Bootstrap for a specific version, go to the main website at the following location, replacing the Word version with the version of Bootstrap you are using: http://getbootstrap.com/<version>/index.html.

Bootstrap alerts in your Splunkdashboard

As a way to start looking through Bootstrap within our example, we will take a look at implementing some of the predefined alert message types. You have probably seen these types of alert used before and we will implement them shortly.

As with the other styles we have been working with, we implement the alerts with the specifically designed class, called in this instance alert. This is then followed by one of the four alert type classes:

- `.alert-success`
- `.alert-info`
- `.alert-warning`
- `.alert-danger`

The data that we have been using is for 2015 and I think that it may be worth using an alert to remind our users of this. Log onto your development environment and we will start working with our raw dashboard code again:

1. As we are working on with the default implementation of Bootstrap, we can move straight to the html directory of our Splunk App:

   cd $SPLUNK_HOME/etc/apps/stock_market/default/data/ui/html/

2. Open the `raw_stock_market_historical_overview_html.html` file in your text or code editor so we can start to make some changes.

3. We are going to use a little bit of animation with our alert that will allow our users to remove the alert after they have read it. We are going to achieve this by adding some external JavaScript in the header of our code that will work directly with the Bootstrap CSS. Start by adding the following two lines just before the end of the header:

   ```
   13      <script src="https://ajax.googleapis.com/
           ajax/libs/jquery/1.12.2/jquery.min.js"></script>
   14      <script src="http://maxcdn.bootstrapcdn.com/
           bootstrap/3.3.6/js/bootstrap.min.js"></script>
   ```

4. We are limited in time to discuss in detail what these files do, but just know that it adds extra JavaScript functionality to our code to ensure that our changes work.

5. We are going to place our alert in the body of our dashboard and specify it just above the `Yahoo Stock Value` heading. Firstly, add in the container class with the following line of code:

```
36    <div class="container">
```

6. Bootstrap requires that each of the site elements that we use from the CSS file be wrapped in the container class.

7. We can then add in the alert class with the following lines of code:

```
37        <div class="alert alert-info fade in"
          style="width:75%;margin-top:18px;">
38            <a href="#" class="close" data-dismiss="alert"
              aria-label="close" >&times;</a>
39            <strong>NOTE!</strong> This stock market data
              for Yahoo is from 2015.
40        </div>
41    </div>
```

8. We are specifying the `alert-info` type, with line 37, and then giving the option to close off the alert if the user wants to dismiss it. We can then specify the text that will be presented as part of the alert.

9. In line 37, although we are using the external CSS class called alert, we can also add in some inline style definitions to change the default text if there was an issue with the color being used by our theme being difficult to see. Internal, external, and inline CSS can be mixed together, but as we stated earlier in this chapter, it is more efficient to set up all our style definitions as an external CSS file.

10. Using CSS that is part of our Splunk installation allows us to work a lot more quickly implementing our changes to our code. Save the changes, refresh the Splunk cache, and reload our dashboard page.

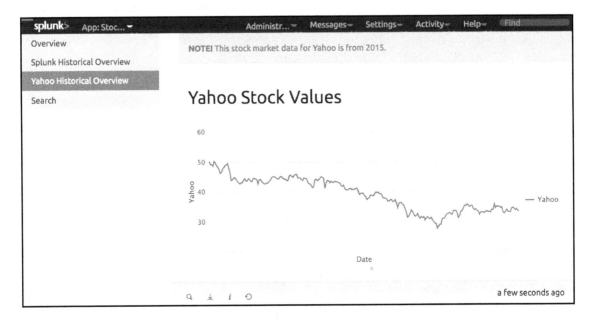

When our page loads, we can see our alert on top of the **Yahoo Stock Values** heading, providing a note to our users that the data is from 2015. As you can see, it was a simple change but added extra functionality to our dashboard. The functionality also allows the user to cancel this alert if needed.

This is a good example of issues being caused by mixing up CSS themes and templates. The alert that we have just implemented, although it provides the user with the ability to close the alert, it is very difficult to see on the United theme. If this were implemented onto our production environment, it would be wise to have this option changed within the code. Color can also cause accessibility issues for disabled users or users who are only using a monochrome display. Make sure to keep this in mind when developing your code.

Bootstrap and dashboard headings

While we are working with Bootstrap CSS, let's also add a proper heading for our dashboard, so people know the Splunk App that they are using. There are many classes to choose from when using Bootstrap, including the jumbotron and page-header classes. Both of these are useful for displaying page headings and banners.

In this part of the chapter, we will quickly add a page-header element from Bootstrap to show our users what dashboard users are actually using. The development of our dashboard is really starting to speed up. We have added the CSS libraries that we are going to use and we have already set up the container class that Bootstrap works with, so it is simply a matter of adding a new div element that will use the page-header element:

1. We should still be in our html directory of our Stock Market Splunk App, and we are going to be working on the `raw_stock_market_historical_overview_html.html` file. So open it up again in your text or code editor.

2. Move down into the body of the HTML code again, and add our page-header element on top of our alert that we had just set up. Add in the following code:

```
38    <div class="page-header";">
39      <h1>Stock Market Splunk App</h1>
40      <p>Utilizing the Bootstrap framework for
        developing responsive Splunk dashboard on the web.</p>
41    </div>
```

3. As you can see, we have used the page-header class and then set up a h1 element for our heading, and then a paragraph underneath explaining what our dashboard does.

4. Save all your changes and reload the Splunk cache. Now view the raw dashboard to see if the new heading is now being displayed on our page:

Your raw dashboard should now display a clear heading with our Splunk App's name and underneath that our nice description of what the Splunk App does.

Bootstrap tool tips

Finally, we want to make a simple change to our raw dashboard that will add in a tool tip and provide our users with the specific search query being run. As you can imagine, Bootstrap makes this pretty easy to implement into our code. Our current heading that shows that we are displaying Yahoo! stock market data is the perfect place that we can add this tool tip.

1. We should still be in our html directory of our Stock Market Splunk App, so once again open the `raw_stock_market_historical_overview_html.html` file with your code or text editor.

2. Our current `h2` element is currently on line 48 and has its own style set up. We will replace it with the following code, which will also bring the heading in line with the **United** theme that we implemented earlier:

```
49        <a href="#" data-toggle="tooltip"
          title="Search Query: source=*yhoostock.csv | chart
          values(Close) AS Yahoo by Date">
          <h2>Yahoo Stock Values</h2></a>
```

3. We use an `a` element to reference the data-toggle item to set up our tool tip with the specified text for the tool tip.

4. Save your changes again and reload the Splunk cache. You will note that our dashboard now has a button to allow the user to view the Splunk search query:

The heading element is now in red, which is in line with the rest of the United theme. When you place your mouse pointer over the heading, you will see the image that we have in the preceding screenshot, where it provides the search query being run inside a tooltip.

Losing our Bootstrap themes

I just want to demonstrate one thing before moving forward, and that is if we lose our Bootstrap theme or it is removed from our environment. This should not impact us too badly, as we can see in the next screenshot. As an example, I have removed the `bootstrap.min.css` file from our static directory in our Stock Market Splunk App. The dashboard has simply loaded all the default Splunk Bootstrap styles instead, but we want to make sure that this does not happen with the apps that we develop.

The documentation provided by Splunk does not go into too much detail when it comes to using the Bootstrap framework or the plugins available within the default installation. You will find more information available through the Bootstrap documentation as it will show you what is available in each of the versions of the framework as well as how to use and implement the plugin in your code.

We have taken our Stock Market Splunk App into a new realm of visualization enhancement and pushed the boundaries of how the Splunk Web Framework is used in presenting data to our users. Even at this point, there are some limitations that are presented to developers and designers when customizing the way that our dashboard both looks and feels. One of the main things that I can think of is that there is an increase in the use of tablets and smart phones for using and accessing these kinds of reports and unfortunately Splunk does not do the best job in providing these dashboards to smaller screens. At the time of writing, there are some experimental plugins that can be used to scale dashboards for different screen sizes, but by default, Splunk does not specifically support this even with the implementation of the Bootstrap framework, which we have been using in this chapter.

Splunk does give you some options to move your data and visualizations into away from Splunk as a platform and allow developers the ability to make further customizations available to the end user. Although we will be finishing up the work that we are doing with this Splunk App on Splunk, we will continue to work with the data and have it hosted on an external web page using SplunkJS.

Summary

We have completely changed the appearance of our raw dashboard in this chapter by using a number of different techniques, all of which utilize CSS. We have done a lot of work in this chapter, starting with a discussion of CSS themes and templates, and implementing a free CSS theme in our raw dashboard. We started to implement our own style definitions onto our example dashboard using both inline and internal style sheets. We then refactored our code and moved our internal definitions into an external CSS file.

Our work then moved on to utilize some of the inbuilt styles and functionality provided to be used within our Splunk installation. We saw that the Splunk Web Framework provides us with a number of professional features that can be implemented easily by experienced web developers. We then examined some specific examples that we implemented in our example Splunk App that specifically used the Bootstrap framework.

In our next chapter, we will start to look at taking our Splunk App away from our Splunk environment by utilizing SplunkJS. We will look directly at setting up external pages that connect and communicate with Splunk to extract and examine data, while allowing developers to host this data on external dashboards.

9

Moving Your App off Splunk with Splunk JS

It has been an amazing journey so far and I hope you've stuck with us until now because the final chapter of this book uses what you have been learning over the rest of the book and takes it to a whole new level. In this chapter, we are going to move from using our Splunk server as a platform for development and move our visualizations and interface onto a standalone web page. We will continue to use the Splunk Web Framework as we want to continue using the data that we have available for our users, but we will use the set of libraries provided through SplunkJS to implement this data on our own website.

This chapter has a lot to cover, but by the end you will hopefully know all about these topics:

- What is SplunkJS and how can it be utilized within our website?
- How to host and set up a website served through Nginx, no longer using Splunk as the platform, and look at some of the dependencies for using SplunkJS
- You will see how to incorporate the SplunkJS code into your external website code
- How to use SplunkJS to connect and communicate with a Splunk Server and set up search managers to extract our data from Splunk
- We will use some of the common libraries within SplunkJS to enhance our websites visual appeal
- Finally, we will take a look at setting up automated testing for our website to help streamline the development process

Once again, you are probably asking why we need to do something like this when we have a perfectly sufficient development and service platform in the shape of our Splunk environment. Well, as discussed towards the end of the last chapter, even with the numerous features that are provided within our Splunkserver, there are still some limitations that cannot be resolved without moving to an externally hosted web environment. There may also be situations where the data that we are collecting will be provided to an external company that they then provide to their customers.

This is where our example Stock Market Splunk App will help, as in this chapter we will use the data that we have collected for our stock market values and provide this data for our external website.

So what is SplunkJS?

SplunkJS is included as part of the Splunk Web Framework to specifically allow web developers to create Splunk style visualizations and dashboards from within their own websites. You can download SplunkJS from the developer site at the following location: `htt p://dev.splunk.com/view/SP-CAAAEWR`.

By adding SplunkJS to your own website code, it provides you with the ability to interact with all the web framework components and enables you to interact with your Splunk data with ease by providing the following:

- It provides all the tools you will need to connect, authenticate, and interact with your Splunkenvironment.
- It gives you the ability to construct search managers to create queries to extract the data you need from Splunk. This data can be used for your external or third-party visualizations and charts.
- SplunkJS provides all the same visualizations that you are used to using in your HTML dashboards, so you can get started setting up your visualizations with ease.

As we have been developing our code with HTML, CSS, and JavaScript, we will continue developing with this framework when using SplunkJS. And if you have been following along so far with our Stock Market Splunk App example, you will see that there are not many more concepts you need to grasp to move on to developing with SplunkJS.

What about the Splunk SDK?

Due to a limit in time and pages, we will not be covering the Splunk **Standard Development Kit (SDK)**. If you have been working with Splunk for some time now, you would be aware that it provides a REST API that external websites are able to interact with and extract data by performing search queries through your API calls. Although you can interact with the REST API directly, you can use the Splunk SDK to interact with the data on Splunk, as they provide a wrapper around the REST API in a number of specific programming languages, including C#, Java, JavaScript, PHP, Python, and Ruby.

The Splunk SDK helps simplify access to the REST API by handling authentication and HTTP requests. For further information on the Splunk SDKs available, please see the developer documentation at the following URL: `http://dev.splunk.com/sdks`.

Host Splunk data outside of Splunk

Let's not waste any more time and get stuck into getting our Splunk data visible outside of our Splunkenvironment. It's a pretty major project and over the next few pages we will need to get the following organized:

- We need to start by setting up a basic website with no real content, using Nginx as a web server. I have used Nginx in this example as it does not use too much processing power and I am familiar with the configurations and its operation. Other web servers can be used, and feel free to use them if you would prefer.
- We are going to set up a proxy connection to our Splunk environment so that we can connect and extract data.
- We are going to install SplunkJS in our external website.
- We are going to test connections with a sample web page that SplunkJS helps us to get started.
- We will then work through setting up our own web dashboard that works directly with our stock market data.

As with the rest of the book, we will step through every part of this project and try to explain each part in as much detail as possible.

Setting up our website

As discussed before, we need to set up our own website being hosted by a web server. In these examples, we will be using Nginx as our web server. Nginx is an open source web server that will run a little better on a lower power CPU, which could be in place in a development environment. There is a large amount of documentation available and it is freely available. The work we are going to do with setting up Nginx to perform the changes we want will be very minor and able to be set up on any other type of web server you may be wanting to use.

1. Log on to your development environment and download and install Nginx on your system. It does not need to be specifically on your development environment, but it will need to communicate with your Splunk server. The following URL will provide you with installation packages and documentation on how to install Nginx for your particular server `https://nginx.org/`. Once you have installed Nginx on your environment and it is running, you need to configure it to serve to a specific location, usually localhost, and on a specific port number:

2. I have installed Nginx on my Macbook, so the configuration file may be located in a different directory than yours, but you need to change to the Nginx configuration file directory:
   - For Mac:

   cd /usr/loca/etc/nginx/

3. For Linux:

   cd /etc/nginx/

4. If you are familiar with setting up web servers, feel free to set it up in a way that suites your needs, but for now, we will set up the web server on the default configuration file. So, open the `nginx.conf` file with your code or text editor.

5. Look for the section that describes our server configuration, which should be at about line 35. By default, your port should be 8080 and the server name should be localhost. Move down a few lines and make sure that the location is set for the directory that your web server is set up for. On my installation, the configuration is as follows:

```
location / {
    root    /usr/local/var/www/html;
    index   index.html index.htm;
}
```

6. Restart the nginx process on your server and you should be able to open a web browser and load the URL: `http://localhost:8080`.

7. The default nginx `index.html` page will be loaded and you browser should show something similar to this screenshot:

Welcome to nginx!

If you see this page, the nginx web server is successfully installed and working. Further configuration is required.

For online documentation and support please refer to nginx.org. Commercial support is available at nginx.com.

Thank you for using nginx.

Interacting with Splunk through the management port

Our standalone website will be able to connect and search Splunk data, but we need to make some changes to the way that our environment is set up so that we can connect to our Splunk servers management port; this is usually on port 8089. Once again, Nginx can help us achieve this by setting up a proxy server to pass a specific URL through to the management port:

1. We should still be logged in to our development environment and in the Nginx configuration directory. We open the `nginx.conf` file with our code or text editor again so that we can add a proxy server onto our environment.

2. My Splunk server is using the domain `splunkdev`, so this is why I am setting up my proxy to this domain. When you make your last change to the `nginx.conf` file, you will need to add the following lines just after your location settings:

```
location /proxy/ {
  proxy_pass https://splunkdev:8089/;
  proxy_ssl_session_reuse off;
}
```

3. This configuration is basically telling Nginx to pass our requests that are being sent to the `/proxy` endpoint onto the proxy URL specified. This will allow our external website to authenticate and communicate with our Splunk server.

Let's get started with SplunkJS

This is where the fun really starts. We are going to download SplunkJS, add it to our working directory for our new web server, and use one of the test web pages to make sure we can connect to our Splunkenvironment:

1. Log back into your development environment, where you have just set up your new web server, and move to the `/tmp` directory.

2. Download SplunkJS in the `/tmp` directory so that you can start working with it. As we stated earlier in this chapter, it can be downloaded from the following URL: `http://dev.splunk.com/view/SP-CAAAEWR`.

3. At the time of writing this book, the version of the download was 1.1. Unzip or uncompress the file you have downloaded and we will move around the parts that we want to use.

4. We want to copy the entire static directory from the file we have just downloaded in our web server directory. Make note that your web server may not be on the same directory that I am using:

```
cp -r /tmp/SplunkJS_Stack/static /usr/local/var/www/html/
```

5. Splunk also gives us some sample web pages that we can use to get started. We are going to use the `test_login.html` web page to verify that we can authenticate and connect to our Splunk server. We will copy this over as well and place it in our web server directory:

```
cp /tmp/SplunkJS_Stack/tests_and_samples/test_login.html
/usr/local/var/www/html/
```

6. We move into our web server directory so that we can adjust the test login page to use our login credentials:

   cd /usr/local/var/www/html/

7. Open the `test_login.html` file with your code or text editor, and we are going to make a minor change. When you open the file, you will notice that there is not much difference from when we were working with dashboards in HTML. We will run through all of the code shortly, but for now move down to the JavaScript section of the code in line 64.

8. This section is where we specify our proxy path and login credentials for our Splunk server that we are going to extract our data from:

```
64     splunkjs.config({
65         proxyPath: '/proxy',
66         scheme: 'https',
67         host: 'splunkdev',
68         port: 8089,
69         authenticate: {username: 'admin', password:
           'changeme'}
70     });
```

9. I have placed the entire block of code in there. But we want to make sure that the username and password are set to a specific user that can access our Splunk environment and our host also reflects the proxy server configurations that we have set up previously.

10. You should not have to reload or restart your Nginx server. You should be able to open a browser and access the web server domain that you have set up previously with the `test_login.html` location:
    `http://localhost:8080/test_login.html`.

11. If you have set up all your credentials correctly and SplunkJS is also downloaded and installed correctly, your browser should be showing a page similar to this one:

Login Tests

Test login with proxy using username/password

This page tests passing a dict to authenticate. It:

- Checks that login succeeds
- Checks that a search manager can get data
- Checks that the username is set

Steps:

No interaction required. If there are no errors and everything is green, it passes.

A table should appear here

count ⬍
10

Messages

Login success

username successfully set!

Manager done

Errors

12. You have just set up your first external website that is serving up Splunk data. The code connects to our Splunk server, authenticates with the username and password, runs multiple searches, and provides an output to our page, including a Splunk visualization in the form of a table. Congratulations, but let's keep moving.

 SplunkJS offers a large number of example pages that can interact directly with your Splunk environment as we have just set up. The examples cover different types of visualizations and Splunk elements to enable you to learn from these examples and then implement in your sites if you need to.

So what if your test page doesn't work?

We are moving into some more advanced areas here, and as a result we have moved pretty fast through the code to try and get it working as quickly as possible. But what if your page is not displaying an image similar to the one shown earlier?

If you haven't worked with a web server such as Nginx, it may be difficult to understand where the issue may be. Your web server has specific logs that you can view as you are testing to try and narrow down where the issue is. The web logs are specified in the `nginx.conf` file that we worked on earlier and will usually be located in the `/var/log/` directory.

If there are any issues with loading CSS, supporting JavaScript, or authenticating with your Splunk server, some of the first places you should be checking are your `access.log` and `error.log` files. You most likely know Splunk already and are most likely indexing these logs as part of your environment.

Let's create our new web page...mobile first

A friend and colleague recently mentioned something to me about web development that has been resonating with me ever since. He told me that web development needs to cater to mobile phones and tablets first as this is where the majority of usage will be driven. So for the web page that we are now going to create, we are going to make sure that it will scale to smaller screen sizes used with mobile phones and tablets. It's going to be pretty easy to achieve this, and while we do it, we are going to give you a full explanation on utilizing SplunkJS along the way.

In the example, we are going to continue using our Stock Market Data, but we will assume that we are providing this data to an independent stock broking firm, who then pass this information to their clients in the form of a website.

Let's start by discussing the code structure of our web page. We are going to run from the top of the script to the bottom, and you will notice that it is very similar to the HTML dashboard code that we were working on in the previous chapter. So the sections should be familiar to you, with some minor tweaks and changes to fit them into our standalone web page. The code will include the following:

- HTML header code, including metadata, CSS, and JavaScript being utilized by the page.
- The actual HTML code that will display our visualizations and text and set up our layout. Remember, mobile first!
- Set up our connection, authentication, and communication with our Splunk environment.
- Load all our required libraries and dependencies for our views, charts, and search managers.
- Set up the code for our search managers to perform our Splunk queries on our stock market data.
- Set up our Splunk visualization elements, which can then be used in the HTML section of the code.

Let us get started with our new website. You need to log on to your development environment, where you now have a working web server and you have Splunk running as well:

1. Move into the directory where all of your code will be hosted. This is the same directory that you placed the `test_login.html` file in. Your directory may differ from my location:

   cd /usr/local/var/www/html/

2. We are going to create a new file for our code, so create a file named `company_site.html` and open it with your code or text editor.

3. We can start by setting up the header:

   ```
   1 <!DOCTYPE html>
   2 <html lang="en">
   3 <head>
   4     <meta charset="utf-8">
   5     <title>Stock Broking Company</title>
   6     <meta name="viewport" content="width=device-width,
          initial-scale=1.0">
   ```

Nothing too difficult here, but make sure you add in line 6 as this will help us change the scale of our page as the size of the browser changes. This will allow us to scale for smartphones and tablets.

4. We can now set up CSS for our page. If we wanted to have our page look like a Splunk dashboard, we would load in the CSS file that is part of the SplunkJS package. In our case, we are going to make our page look a little different from the Splunk styles, so we will load in the most recent version of Bootstrap as well as some extra JavaScript libraries to help with visualization of our content:

```
7 <!-- Latest compiled and minified CSS -->
8     <link rel="stylesheet"
      href="http://maxcdn.bootstrapcdn.com/bootstrap
      /3.3.6/css/bootstrap.min.css">
9     <!-- jQuery library -->
10     <script
      src="https://ajax.googleapis.com/ajax/libs/jquery/
      1.12.2/jquery.min.js"></script>
11     <!-- Latest compiled JavaScript -->
12     <script
      src="http://maxcdn.bootstrapcdn.com/bootstrap/
      3.3.6/js/bootstrap.min.js"></script>
13 </head>
```

5. We can now start to set up the body of the html code. The following code is using the jumbotron div container for our heading, which is available in Bootstrap. This will allow our heading to size and scale depending on the size of the browser window:

```
15 <body>
16 <!-- html section of the code -->
17 <div class="container">
18   <div class="jumbotron">
19       <h1>Stock Broking Company</h1>
20       <p>We specialize in providing you with Splunk
          Stock Market Data</p>
21   </div>
22 </div>
```

6. We can now set up a grid to allow us to import single-value data from our Splunk environment:

```
24 <div class="container-fluid">
25       <div class="row">
26           <div class="col-sm-6">
27               <div class="panel panel-default
```

```
                        text-center">
28                          <div class="panel-
                        heading">
29                              <h1>Yahoo -
                        Highest Close Value</h1>
30                          </div>
```

We use the container-fluid class; it will scale with our browser size. We then open up our row and use the `col-sm-6` class for our column value; it will set up our column to expand to halfway through our screen.

7. Our code can now set up our element details. You will notice that line 32 uses an ID of `maxsingle1`, which is the visualization element we are going to set up shortly to display the maximum closing value for the Yahoo! stock through 2015:

```
31 <div class="panel-body">
32                  <h4><div id="maxsingle1"></div></h4>
33                      </div>
34                      <div class="panel-footer">
35                      <h3>For Financial Year 2015</h3>
36                          </div>
37                  </div>
38              </div>
```

8. The next lines of code will do the same thing but in a separate column; it will use a different visualization that will provide the average value of Yahoo! stock market closing values:

```
39      <div class="col-sm-6">
40      <div class="panel panel-default
        text-center">
41      <div class="panel-heading">
42      <h1>Yahoo - Average Close Value</h1>
43      </div>
44      <div class="panel-body">
45      <h4><div   id="avgsingle2"></div></h4>
46      </div>
47      <div class="panel-footer">
48      <h3>For Financial Year 2015</h3>
49                              </div>
50                          </div>
51                  </div>
52          </div>
53 </div>
```

We also nicely close off all our `div` elements for our row containers.

9. We can now set up a separate row that will span the entire browser page and we will place it at the bottom of our single-value data:

```
55 <div class="container">
56          <div class="row">
57                  <div class="span12">
58                          <h2>Yahoo Financial Year - Closing
                            Values by Day</h2>
59                          <div id="yearchart"></div>
60                  </div>
61          </div>
62 </div>
```

The code uses the ID of `yearchart`, which is also a visualization that we are going to set up shortly.

Authenticating with your Splunkenvironment

Our code so far looks very similar to the code from the HTML dashboard that we have been working on in the previous chapters. One major difference that you need to note is that we need to set up authentication with our Splunk environment to allow communication to take place. In our previous chapters, this was not an issue as we were using our Splunk environment as our development platform, but now when we move our web pages off Splunk, this needs to be taken into consideration.

This is one of the great features of SplunkJS. By using the `config.js` JavaScript file, it allows us to easily authenticate without the need for any complicated coding. It's now time to implement our authentication as part of our website, so let's continue with our coding:

1. We should already have our `company_site.html` file open and we can start by moving down to the bottom of the file, where we will start to add the JavaScript section of our code:

```
64 <!-- JavaScript section of the code -->
65 <script src="../static/splunkjs/config.js"></script>
66 <script>
```

Our code has a dependency on SplunkJS-specifically on the `config.js` file. This is where we have added this as a source for our code to be able to use.

2. We can now use the config function within our code and the following lines set up our configuration to then authenticate with our Splunk environment:

```
67 splunkjs.config({
68        proxyPath: '/proxy',
69        scheme: 'https',
70        host: 'splunkdev',
71        port: 8089,
72        authenticate: {username: 'admin', password:
           'notchangeme'}
73    });
74 </script>
```

It looks a little simple, but that's all you need to do to now communicate and query data from your Splunk environment. You will remember that these credentials match the proxy server that we set up in Nginx earlier.

In the preceding code, we are providing our username and password in plain text, which does bring up some security issues. We have done this to display the ease of connecting to our Splunk server, but in a publically accessible website, we would ensure that our username and passwords were encrypted or add a username and password HTML input to allow the user to enter their details when needed.

3. If you remember in our previous chapters when we worked with the HTML dashboards, there were a number of libraries that we needed to use to implement our search queries and our visualizations. We set up the baseUrl location so that we can simplify the loading of all the required libraries that we needed:

```
76 <script>
77 require.config({baseUrl: "../static/"});
78 </script>
```

4. We can now provide a list of all the libraries that we need to use and associate them back with variables, which can then be used in our functions later in the code:

```
80 <script>
81    require([
82        "jquery",
83        "splunkjs/mvc/searchmanager",
84        "splunkjs/splunk",
85        "splunkjs/ready!",
86        "splunkjs/mvc/singleview",
87        "splunkjs/mvc/chartview",
```

```
88    ], function(
89        $,
90        SearchManager,
91        sdk,
92        mvc,
93        SingleView,
94        ChartView)
95    {
```

The number of functions may seem a little small compared to our previous work, but remember that we do not need to worry about all the Splunk-related libraries that are needed for things such as the header and footer specific for Splunk HTML dashboards.

5. This now allows us to set up the code to create search managers for our queries and our visualizations. Our first search manager is in the following code:

```
97  var manager = new SearchManager({
98   id: "search1",
99   search: "source="\*yhoostock.csv" | chart
     max(Close) AS close | eval Yahoo=round(close,2) | table
     Yahoo",
100               earliest_time: "-1y@y"
101          });
```

As you can see, it is the same as we would implement a search manager in a HTML dashboard. The preceding code will provide the highest closing value for our previous year.

6. We only have one of our searches set up. Let's now implement the search managers for the rest of the queries that we want to run. We need to have a query to provide the average closing value, and we will also set up a timechart query for our chart, which we are going to place at the bottom of our web page:

```
103 var manager = new SearchManager({
104   id: "search2",
105   search: "source="\*yhoostock.csv" | chart
      avg(Close) AS close | eval Yahoo=round(close,2) | table
      Yahoo",
106               earliest_time: "-1y@y"
107          });
108
109       var manager = new SearchManager({
110           id: "search3",
111           search: "source="\*yhoostock.csv" | timechart
              span=1d values(Close) AS YahooClose",
```

```
112                earliest_time: "-1y@y"
113            });
```

7. We can now set up visualizations for our searches. We have two searches that would use a `SingleView` visualization if we were implementing this in Splunk directly. As a result, we will utilize the `SingleView` function that we imported as part of SplunkJS:

```
115 // Single View and Charts
116         var single1 = new SingleView({
117             id:"maximum-single",
118             managerid: "search1",
119             el: $("#maxsingle1")
120         }).render();
121
122         var single2 = new SingleView({
123             id:"average-single2",
124             managerid: "search2",
125             el: $("#avgsingle2")
126         }).render();
```

Simply, we create a variable for each of the visualizations using the `SingleView` function. We use one of the searches that we defined in the previous code and then provide it with an element ID (`el`), which can then be used as part of our HTML div elements.

8. The interesting thing is that JavaScript allows us to use SplunkJS functions without the need to assign them to a variable. Let's try that out in the next part of the code, where we want to set up a chart element that will be displayed at the bottom of our page:

```
128 new ChartView({
129             managerid: 'search3',
130             el: $('#yearchart').append('<div></div>'),
131             "charting.legend.placement": "bottom"
132         }).render();
```

As you can see, we can specify the use of `ChartView` without needing to assign it to a variable.

9. Finally, we can close off our code, including the `script`, `body`, and `html` elements:

```
134 });
135 </script>
136
137 </body>
138 </html>
```

10. Save your file, and because we have Nginx already running, there is no need to reload the Splunkcache or anything like that. It is now the moment of truth. We have put a lot of work into our new company website, and if you have set up your web server with the domain of localhost, you can go to the following URL and see if your page loads: `http://localhost:8080/company_site.html`.

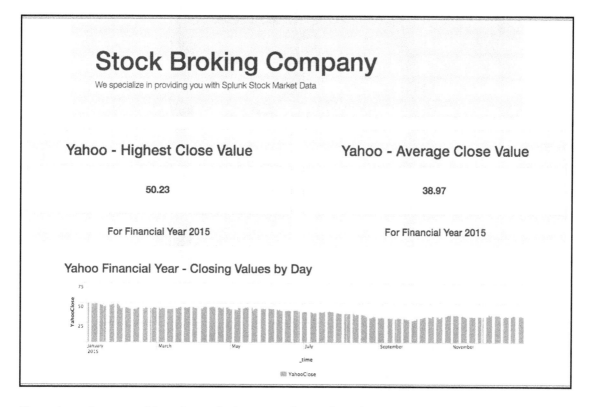

If you have been working through the examples so far, I hope you're excited with what we have come up with. Our stock broking website has come up looking nice and clean, and I think gives users some excellent insights into the Yahoo! historical stock market values over 2015.

We have been able to use Bootstrap styles to make a clean and user-friendly interface. We extracted values directly from our Splunk index using the search managers that we created in our code, and finally, we used a Splunk visualization in the form of a chart to show the historical closing stock market values over one year.

The question we need to ask though is: does this work with a mobile browser on a smartphone or tablet? If we use a smartphone emulator, we see can that our jumbotron heading will scale to the size of our browser, our maximum and average stock value elements will move and display underneath each other, and our chart will fit in nicely down the bottom of the web page:

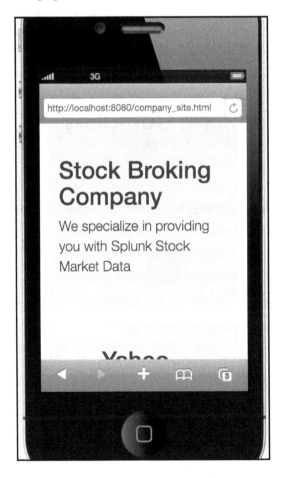

The emulator doesn't give us the full details of how the page is scaled for a smaller browser.

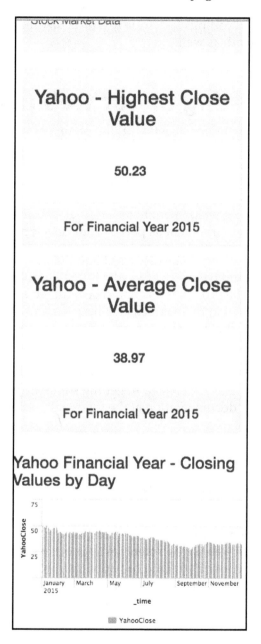

As you can see, when we shrink the width of the browser, the rows that we set up to display the highest and average closing values are now stacked on top of each other to fit into our smaller screen. The headings also scale to a nicer size, and our chart at the bottom of the screen fits into the width as well.

Automated testing of our web page

Although we only have a few moments left working on this example, I would like to take this opportunity to discuss testing of your Splunk Apps. As we know, if you are still using Splunk as your development platform, you will be generating internal log files that will be indexed automatically and available to query with Splunk and be able to set up alerting around any errors that you may experience. When your experience progresses, especially when you start to move your development to an external website, it could be wise for you to set up an automated test environment as part of your development process.

Your testing is something that should be discussed and planned when your initial project planning occurs, as you should have a clear idea of how the process should be. As features and bug fixes are added to the project, tests should be outlined and set up before the development work occurs so that there is a clear consensus on when the task is considered to be complete. In the last part of this chapter, we will have a look at Selenium to set up a quick, automated test to ensure that our company's web page loads.

We are going to very briefly touch on this subject to give you an idea on how to set up something like this, but if you are interested in getting some further information, you should look at the Selenium documentation at the following location: `http://www.seleniu mhq.org/docs/`.

In the following example, we are going to be working from our command line to install and run our tests. If you are not working on either Linux or Mac, please consult the documentation for details on installation on your environment: `http://selenium-python. readthedocs.io/installation.html`.

If you have not used Selenium before, it is a scripting tool that allows testers and developers to automate interaction with web pages. Selenium supports multiple languages, but in the next example we are going to use Python to code our test, as we are able to use the `unittest` library that comes by default with our installation of Python. As long as you have Python already installed on your development environment, you will be able to use `easy_install` to add Selenium into your environment. The following command will install it for you:

```
sudo easy_install selenium
```

I have also found that the default Firefox browser does have some issues with newer versions of the application, so I have been using `ChromeDriver` in my Selenium tests. To download the latest version of ChromeDriver to use as part of our example, go to the following URL: `https://sites.google.com/a/chromium.org/chromedriver/downloads`.

Writing a simple test

For our example, we will write a simple test that will verify that our company website page loads and shows the correct title that we have coded in our HTML header. We log back into our development server, where we have our web server set up:

1. We are going to write our test in the same directory as our HTML code, so start by moving into the html directory:

   cd /usr/local/var/www/html/

2. Create a new file called `selenium_test.py` and open it with your code or text editor.

3. If you are not familiar with coding in Python, it is not too complex and is very similar to JavaScript. Start by adding the following code, which will add the specific dependencies and modules we need for our test:

```
1 import unittest
2 import time
3 from selenium import webdriver
4 from selenium.webdriver.common.keys import Keys
```

> The first two lines import built-in Python modules. unittest is a test framework, while the time module will help us slow down the commands in our script. Lines 3 and 4 import specific modules as part of Selenium, which we installed a few moments ago.

> If you have not used Python before, be careful with the whitespace that you use in your code. Other languages may define blocks of code using brackets or braces. Python uses indentation and whitespace to define blocks of code. If you decide to use tabs or spaces while indenting code, make sure you stay consistent across all of your code. An image of the entire code and its indentation has been added at the end of this section.

4. We are going to set up our test as a Class within our Python script:

```
6 class CompanySiteTest(unittest.TestCase):
7
8 def setUp(self):
9 self.driver =
  webdriver.Chrome('/usr/local/bin/chromedriver')
```

   The first line creates the class, which is going to use `unittest` as its framework. The setup initializes our webdriver and in this example.

5. The main function of this code can now be set up, with our function being called `test_load_company_site`. You can see that it loads our webdriver and then opens the company web page. We have a sleep for 3 seconds in line 14 to allow the user enough time to see what is happening:

```
11      def test_load_company_site(self):
12          driver = self.driver
13      driver.get("http://localhost:8080/company_site.html")
14              time.sleep(3)
```

6. We then can add an assert call to verify that the title of our website is correct and we'll show an error if this is not correct:

```
15      self.assertIn("Stock Brocking Company",
        driver.title)
16      assert "No results found." not in
        driver.page_source
```

7. Let's set up a second function to test if there is any content in the page as well:

```
18      def test_verify_text(self):
19              driver = self.driver
20      driver.get("http://localhost:8080/company_site.html")
21          self.assertIn("Yahoo - Highest Close Value",
            driver.page_source)
22              assert "No text found in page." not in
                driver.page_source
```

   This will do the same thing as our previous function, except that it will test for one of our headings in the body of the HTML code.

8. Our final function in our code will then close off the driver that we created to set up our tests:

```
24          def tearDown(self):
```

```
25                          self.driver.close()
```

9. Finally, we can add in a way for our main function to be run when we start up the script:

```
27 if __name__ == "__main__":
28          unittest.main()
```

10. Your completed Python code should look similar to this screenshot:

```
 1 import unittest
 2 import time
 3 from selenium import webdriver
 4 from selenium.webdriver.common.keys import Keys
 5
 6 class CompanySiteTest(unittest.TestCase):
 7
 8      def setUp(self):
 9          self.driver = webdriver.Chrome('/usr/local/bin/chromedriver')
10
11      def test_load_company_site(self):
12          driver = self.driver
13          driver.get("http://localhost:8080/company_site.html")
14          time.sleep(3)
15          self.assertIn("Stock Brocking Company", driver.title)
16          assert "No results found." not in driver.page_source
17
18      def test_verify_text(self):
19          driver = self.driver
20          driver.get("http://localhost:8080/company_site.html")
21          self.assertIn("Yahoo - Highest Close Value", driver.page_source)
22          assert "No text found in page." not in driver.page_source
23
24      def tearDown(self):
25          self.driver.close()
26
27 if __name__ == "__main__":
28      unittest.main()
29
```

11. Save all your changes and make sure that Nginx or your web server is running, as the test will not work otherwise.

12. The test can be run from the command line with the following command:

```
python selenium_test.py -v
```

I have added the −v option as part of running the script as it will show you the exact class and functions that are being run. You will notice that the script will pause for 3 seconds just after the page is loaded and then perform the test, hopefully with an okay result. Your output should look similar to this:

```
MacBook-Pro:html user$ python selenium_test.py -v
test_load_company_site (__main__.CompanySiteTest) ... ok
test_verify_text (__main__.CompanySiteTest) ... ok
-------------------------------------------------------------
---------
Ran 2 tests in 6.229s
```

As you can see, we have been able to chain tests together and create more functions within our script.

 Both Chrome and Firefox come with developer tools that allow you so see the specific elements that are highlighted on your web interface. In our example, we searched for text in our page source, but Selenium allows you to identify specific HTML elements and CSS ID values.

Considerations when testing

Our example was only basic; automated tests can be as complex as you need them to be, including tests for the data values that you have displayed on your page. As well as making sure you have a working Splunkserver in your test environment that your application can connect with, you will also need to make sure that you have data available for our standalone web page to load. This may mean having a small sample of data that your Selenium test can verify as being correct for basic tests, but then a mirror of the production indexes to verify that there are no issues using production data.

If you have worked in development teams before you might also be familiar with build tools such as Jenkins or Bamboo. Using these tools along with hosting your repository on GitHub would allow you to automate the entire process. Linking your build tool to GitHub, you would be able to continuously check if changes have been pushed to a specific branch, then grabbing that code, building your website or Splunkpackage, deploying these changes to our test environment, and then finally running our Selenium tests across our new deployment.

Our Stock Market Splunk App has moved into a state that is providing valuable and usable insights to our users, while our new standalone website is now serving data from our Splunk environment as well. The website we created in this chapter can easily be presented to a client as a first iteration. We have been able to move away from Simple XML and start to code our interface with HTML, CSS, and JavaScript on both our Splunk platform and via a web server. We have limited the actual work with the specific stock market data as we have tried to focus more on the delivery of our visualizations and interfaces to our users. The Splunk Web Framework has enabled us to use familiar tools, styles, and frameworks that most web developers would be comfortable with and start to become productive as quickly as possible.

Summary

In this chapter, we covered a lot of topics and a lot of code. We discussed how we can use SplunkJS to utilize the power of our data that we have indexed in Splunk and provide this information to users through external web pages. We discussed some of the dependencies that are needed to move your development away from using Splunk as your development platform including the use of Nginx to set up a web server and proxy server.

We then moved on to the code of our new website and implemented a page that would scale across different devices, including smart phones and tablets. We moved step-by-step setting up our new web page using both SplunkJS and external web frameworks to help streamline our coding and enable us to provide a user friendly and elegant web interface. We finally looked at setting up automated testing within our development process to ensure that our code can move from development, to test, and then to production with as minimal chance for errors as possible. We also discussed some of the development tools that are available for use to help streamline the process.

We have now come to the end of this book and hope that I have been able to provide you with examples and information that are not just interesting and engaging but also a little bit different to try and give you an idea of just how powerful Splunk can actually be. The Splunk Web Framework can be used as a complete development platform to rapidly create engaging and user-friendly reports and interfaces to information that needs to be provided to your users.

Index

www.ingramcontent.com/pod-product-compliance
Lightning Source LLC
Chambersburg PA
CBHW060536060326
40690CB00017B/3511